Forties & Fifties
POPULAR JEWELRY

Styled For You

Roseann Ettinger

with
Price
Guide

Schiffer Publishing Ltd

77 Lower Valley Road, Atglen, PA 19310

Dedication

To my newest jewel, Alexandra,
Born April 7, 1992.

Acknowledgments

Thank you Ceil for another dream come true. Special thanks to Alan Boisvert for being so kind to lend me his computer to finish this book. I would also like to thank my mother and father, Marie and Vito Rodino for constantly supporting me in all my endeavors. Thank you, Marlene Franchetti, for allowing us to photograph some of your favorite pieces of jewelry. And again to my mother for the use of some of hers. To all the great people at Schiffer Publishing, again I thank you for all your help and enthusiasm. Last but not least to my son, Clint and my daughter, Amber, for helping to take care of Alexandra, my baby, so that I could have time to work on this book.

Flower necklace made of gold-plated metal with rhinestone accents, unmarked.

Title Page photo:
Transparent and translucent to-paz-colored glass stones used in combination form this lovely brace-let and earrings set, unmarked, circa 1950s.

Printed in America.
ISBN: 0-88740-560-6

Published by Schiffer Publishing, Ltd.
77 Lower Valley Road
Atglen, PA 19310
Please write for a free catalog.
This book may be purchased from the publisher.
Please include $2.95 postage.
Try your bookstore first.

We are interested in hearing from authors
with book ideas on related subjects.

Contents

Brass, glass and plastic were utilized to create this Victorian Revival demi-parure, circa 1950s.

Preface

The demand for costume jewelry, whether it be fashion jewelry or novelty jewelry, did not die in the 1940s when World War II became a reality. Obviously, methods of manufacture and some of the materials used had to change because of restrictions during the war, but the jewelry that was manufactured or hand-made had exceptional quality in workmanship and design. The same held true for fine or "real" jewelry.

This book will take you further on the tour that started in my earlier book, **Popular Jewelry 1840-1940**. It is intended to aid the reader in identifying the jewelry styles popular from World War II to 1960.

Jewelry by *Karen Lynne* advertised in the Jack Kellmer Company catalog in 1957.

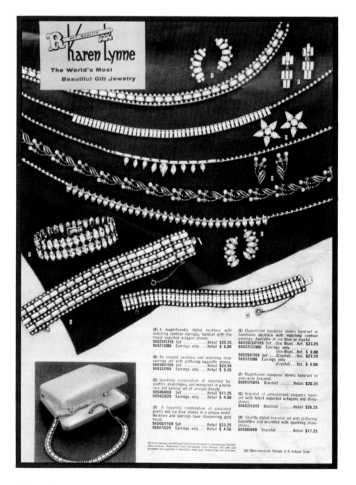

Dazzling stone-set jewelry by *Karen Lynne* offered for sale in 1957.

Introduction

I have been a jewelry fanatic since I was a little girl. My mother and father used to call me a "Gypsy" because I was always playing with jewelry or asking relatives to clean out their jewelry boxes for me. There was a costume jewelry and gift shop in my hometown where my mother took me every Saturday. When I walked into this glamourous shop, I felt as though I was in heaven just gazing at all the jewelry and accessories that sparkled and glittered. We could never afford to buy anything, however, because the jewelry was expensive, even though it was only costume jewelry. It was not like the jewelry that was for sale in the 5&10-cent stores; it was different. At the time, however, no explanations were needed. All I would say to my mother was that I wanted a store like that when I grow up -it was my dream store!

As the years went on, however, my love of jewelry was put on the back burner so that I could pursue other interests. I wanted to be a school teacher so I went to college to reach that goal. I received my degree and taught school for a while but I knew there was something waiting for me that had nothing to do with writing lesson plans. When my first child was born, I realized I wanted to go into business for myself and take my child to work with me. I could not do that being a school teacher. The idea of opening a little business selling antique jewelry just popped into my mind one day and that started my quest on a learning trail that has been filled with joy ever since. That was over fifteen years ago.

After I had been in business for about eight years, my husband, who was an officer in the United States Army, had to serve a tour of duty in Korea. I moved back home and within a week asked my mother if she wanted to go to that jewelry store that we used to frequent every Saturday in my youth. Sadly, she told me that the store had closed a few years earlier. I couldn't believe it and was very disappointed. I also found out that the woman who owned the store was still alive and my father knew her husband. I was estatic to think that maybe some of that great jewelry was tucked away somewhere in my hometown. After a few weeks, contact was made. I found out that the store was closed in the late 1970s and everything was packed up and stored away. I could not believe that I might be able to see some of those great pieces of jewelry that made such an impression on me as a child. I made an appointment with the woman and she agreed to meet with me to talk about the jewelry. I told her that I had been in business for a few years and that I was always on the lookout for some interesting articles for my own store. I reminded her that my mother had taken me into her store when I was a child and that I had always dreamed of having a store

Clip cast in sterling silver, plated in gold and set with molded faux sapphires. The flower basket is further enhanced with clear rhinestones, marked *Trifari*.

Dress clip made of rhodium-plated metal set with simulated carved rubies, emeralds and sapphires. This type of jewelry was extremely fashionable in the 1930s and 1940s. Fine jewelers like Cartier provided the inspiration for mass-produced reproductions to find their way into department stores.

Dress clip set with diamonds and carved rubies, emeralds and sapphires as advertised in *Harper's Bazaar* in March, 1940. The dress clip was the most popular jewelry article made in the 1930s. The vogue lasted well into the next decade and costume jewelry manufacturers copied fine versions such as this one pictured and made them in less expensive materials.

Clip made in the shape of a horn of plenty cast in base metal with a rhodium plating and set with simulated ruby stones, round and baguette rhinestones. The brooch is also made of rhodium-plated base metal and set with simulated rubies and smaller rhinestone accents, circa 1935-1940.

like hers when I grew up. It turned out that she had packed away everything in her store in a hurry without ever having a "Going Out of Business Sale." She had sold some of the inventory over the years, but not that much. To make this long story short, I ended up buying her inventory of fashion jewelry and jeweled accessories. I even bought her showcases that were custom made in the 1950s. It was like everything was there just waiting for me. I was thrilled.

The woman told me that her store opened in 1953. Ironically, that was the year I was born. She also told me that the store closed in 1978. That was the year that my first child was born and the year I decided to go into business. Coincidence.

The majority of the jewelry that dates from the 1950s which was photographed for this book came from the store I just mentioned. When I bought the inventory, being old store stock, most of it retained some of its original packaging. For instance, the earrings were still on their original cards, necklaces and bracelets still had original tags. The jewelry was never worn. Some of the designer pieces from the early 1950s were only identified by the tags that were still attached to them. They were not marked any other way. A tremendous amount of jewelry that was manufactured back then left the factory in that condition. Not all designer jewelry is actually stamped and it annoys me, not only as an author, but as a dealer in antique and vintage jewelry, that some dealers and collectors will only buy a piece of jewelry that is marked and snub their noses at a piece that is not. A tremendous amount of jewelry was made by unknowns, and another abundant supply that may have been made by a sought-after designer but bears no identifying marks. I appreciate the quality and the workmanship of a piece of vintage fashion jewely whether it is marked or not. I'll look at the piece first, get to know it and like it, then I'll ask its name!

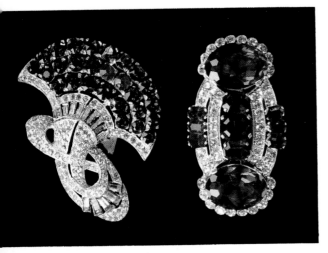

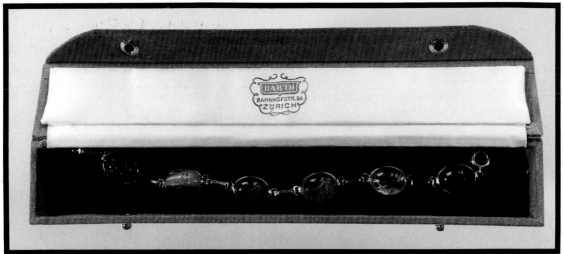

Bracelet made of 14kt gold with six genuine carved stone scarabs in original presentation box, marked *BARTH BAHNHOFSTR. 94 ZURICH.*

Right:

Scarab jewelry, popular in the 1920s, made a come back again in the 1950s. Featured in this 1957 catalog are bracelets, earrings, cuff links and tie bars made of 14K solid gold or gold-filled mountings and set with genuine imported stones by Russel Jewelry Manufacturing Company of Philadelphia.

Opposite page bottom right:
Aquamarine teardrop pin by *Mermod-Jaccard-King.* This brooch sold for $500 in 1940.

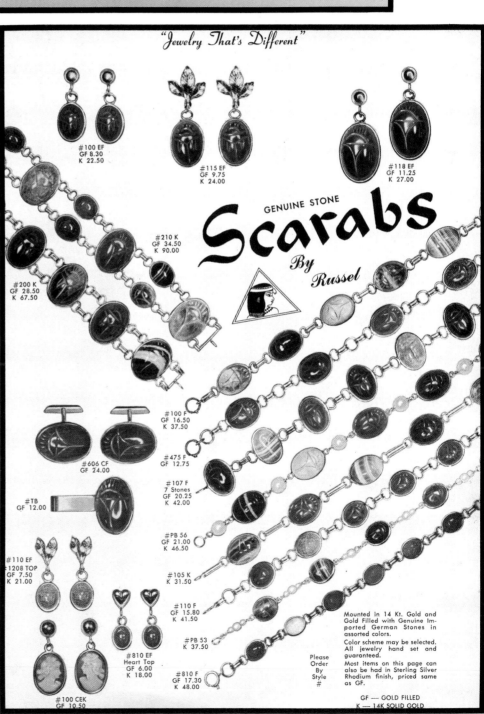

"Jewelry That's Different"

#100 EF
GF 8.30
K 22.50

#115 EF
GF 9.75
K 24.00

#118 EF
GF 11.25
K 27.00

GENUINE STONE
Scarabs
By Russel

#210 K
GF 34.50
K 90.00

#200 K
GF 28.50
K 67.50

#606 CF
GF 24.00

#TB
GF 12.00

#110 EF
1208 TOP
GF 7.50
K 21.00

#100 CEK
GF 10.50

#810 EF
Heart Top
GF 6.00
K 18.00

#100 F
GF 16.50
K 37.50

#475 F
GF 12.75

#107 F
7 Stones
GF 20.25
K 42.00

#PB 56
GF 21.00
K 46.50

#105 K
K 31.50

#110 F
GF 15.80
K 41.50

#PB 53
K 37.50

#810 F
GF 17.30
K 48.00

Please
Order
By
Style
#

Mounted in 14 Kt. Gold and Gold Filled with Genuine Imported German Stones in assorted colors.

Color scheme may be selected. All jewelry hand set and guaranteed.

Most items on this page can also be had in Sterling Silver Rhodium finish, priced same as GF.

GF — GOLD FILLED
K — 14K SOLID GOLD

Palladium is a metallic element, closely resembling platinum that was used for fine jewelry manufacture during World War II. This ad in *Seventeen* magazine shows that the metal was still being used in December of 1948.

During the 1930s, costume jewelry began to take on a new light with the help of Coco Chanel and Elsa Schiaparelli who designed jewelry with glass stones -not precious stones- as costume jewelry that was meant to be worn to compliment a wardrobe. This was the beginning of a new era in "faux" jewelry that appealed to a larger spectrum of buyers. It appealed to the working class as well as those who once frowned upon "fake" jewelry.

Geometric metal jewelry, first popular in the 1920s and 1930s, known as "modern" was again popular in the 1940s and termed "tailored". A slight transformation occurred with the latter type which was, at times, designed with geometric and rococo influences used in combination. The 1940s tailored jewelry was the perfect accessory for padded shoulder suits and dresses made with its fine jewelry look of polished gold-plated sterling silver but completely void of stone ornamentation.

Prior to World War II, Europe provided the majority of the inspiration that American designers and manufacturers needed. This isolation created a new environment from which new ideas were made. Inspirations were drawn from other areas and sources, particularly local customs, Mexican and American Indian cultures, Hollywood, art and the war itself. During the war, Americans had to rely on their own creative genius.

World War Two

Many factories throughout America that had been manufacturing jewelry began producing war-related items. The government put restrictions on certain metals including platinum and copper. For fine jewelry, palladium was used because platinum was restricted. Although palladium looked like platinum, it tarnished, yet it was not as expensive. In February of 1943, gold jewelry with a greenish cast became more popular than gold jewelry with a reddish cast because the red tint came from copper which was scarce. The greenish cast came from silver which was not scarce.

For costume jewelry, white metal and brass were restricted so sterling silver was substituted during the war. Certain designers, Miriam Haskell in particular, used Bohemian (Czech), wooden and plastic beads to creatively produce their fashionable hand-made jewelry. The hungry population, looking for something to take their minds off their troubles, did not starve because of a lack of jewelry during the war. There was plenty to choose from in all styles and price ranges.

This hat advertisement from 1940 which was pictured in *Harper's Bazaar* is a good illustration showing the large scale jewelry that was worn at that time.

Gold Plated

Sterling silver was used tremendously during the 1940s. Large brooches were cast in sterling silver and many times plated in yellow or rose gold. Rhodium-plated jewelry was also popular as well as gold-filled metal jewelry. Designers, manufacturers, wholesale and retail distributors advertised their "smart, modern costume jewelry." In 1944, Sears offered "Jeweled Brooches of Heirloom Quality". A small paragraph in the catalog was devoted to describe these treasures. It read:

> With the final touch of beautiful jewelry, a woman's costume takes on individuality, compels attention and admiration. These exquisite brooches are designed for the discriminating woman who appreciates the pleasure of owning-the thrill of wearing-the finest quality jewelry.

> Precious metal-durable gold-plated sterling silver-is cast into a graceful form, polished and buffed; then hand-set with jewel-cut simulated stones of such beauty it is hard to believe they are not genuine gems. A brooch of this enduring quality is a wise investment.

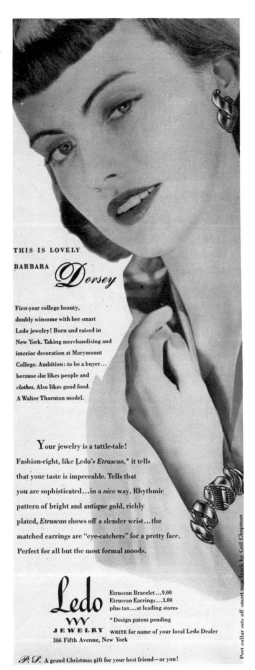

Ledo jewelry advertised in *Seventeen* in December of 1948.

Tailored bracelet and choker necklace made of brass with a gold wash, both marked *Coro*.

Goldtone link jewelry by *Monet* advertised for sale in 1947.

The "Sari" necklace by *Monet* retailed for $15.00 in 1947. The link bracelet retailed for $7.50, the chain bracelet sold for $4.00 while the earrings were also $7.50. A very similar necklace made by *Monet* called the "Cellini" necklace was advertised for sale in 1952.

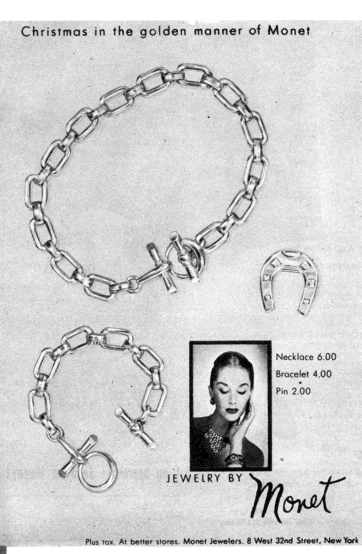

Christmas in the golden manner of Monet

Necklace 6.00
Bracelet 4.00
Pin 2.00

JEWELRY BY *Monet*

Plus tax. At better stores. Monet Jewelers. 8 West 32nd Street, New York

"Sari" the new necklace

for glamour throughout the day—

in the golden manner of *Monet*

Tailored earrings made of gold-plated metal and set with teardrop rhinestones, marked *Trifari*.

Gold Plated 11

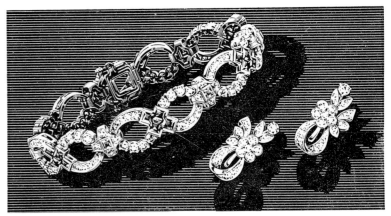

EMERALD AND DIAMOND BRACELET $ 5300.
PAIR OF DIAMOND EARRINGS   1200.

Matched set consisting of necklace, bracelet and earrings made with gold electroplated interlocking links set with fancy cut Austrian crystal stones, marked *Mazer Bros*, circa 1950s.

14 KT. GOLD, RUBY AND DIAMOND NECKLACE $ 1275.

Tiffany & Company provided inspiration for many costume jewelry manufacturers and designers. This advertisement from 1946 shows similarities between the designs in fine jewelry and those which were rendered in less expensive materials.

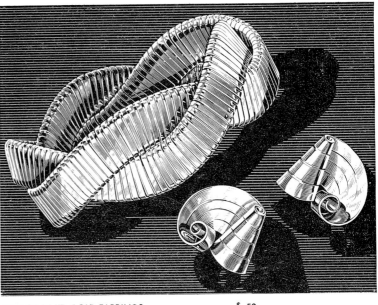

PAIR OF 14 KT. GOLD EARRINGS $ 50.
14 KT. GOLD BRACELET   365.

12 Gold Plated

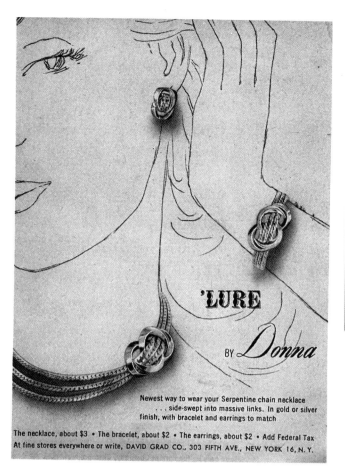

Serpentine chain jewelry by *Donna*
advertised for sale in 1947.

Octagon-shaped lavender glass
stones are framed with gold-filled
leaves to form this pretty necklace
and earring set, marked *Van Dell*.

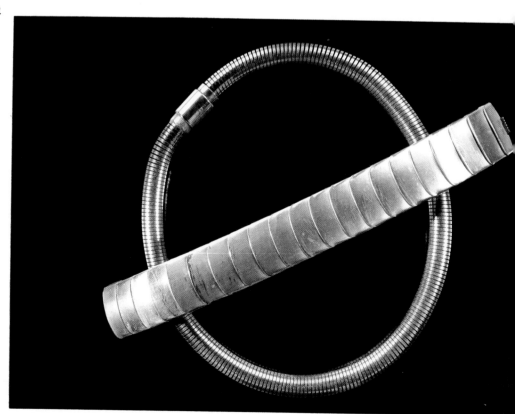

Flexible snake choker and segmented bracelet made of gold-
washed brass, unmarked, circa
1940s.

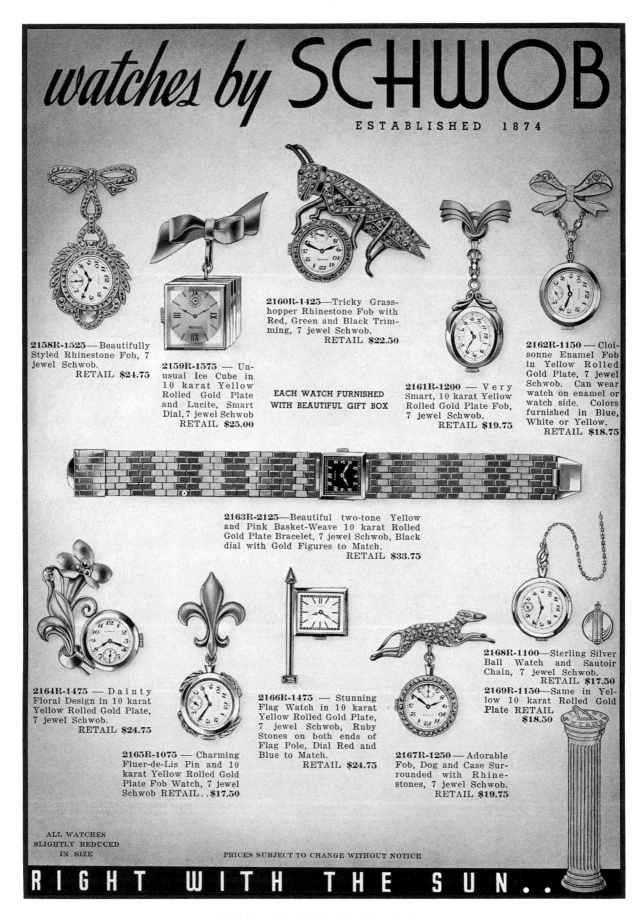

Watches by *Schwob* offered for sale in 1942 from Carson Pirie Scott & Company.

Lapel watch advertised in *Vogue*,
November 1, 1946.

Lapel watch made of 14K gold
formed into a bow, circa 1940s.

Extremely unusual gold-filled coil
bracelet and watch/locket combination. The watch, perched on a
clear Lucite pedestal, is facing in
one direction while the locket, also
perched on Lucite, is facing in the
other direction. The watch mechanism is marked *Imperial*, circa
1940s.

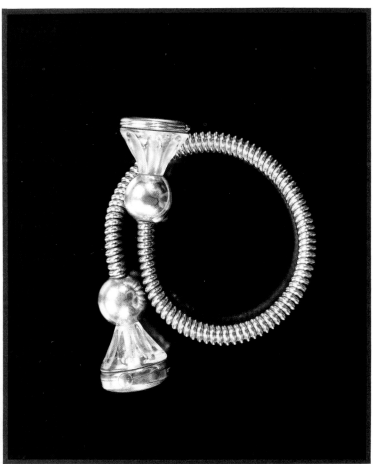

A different view of the combination
bracelet watch/locket.

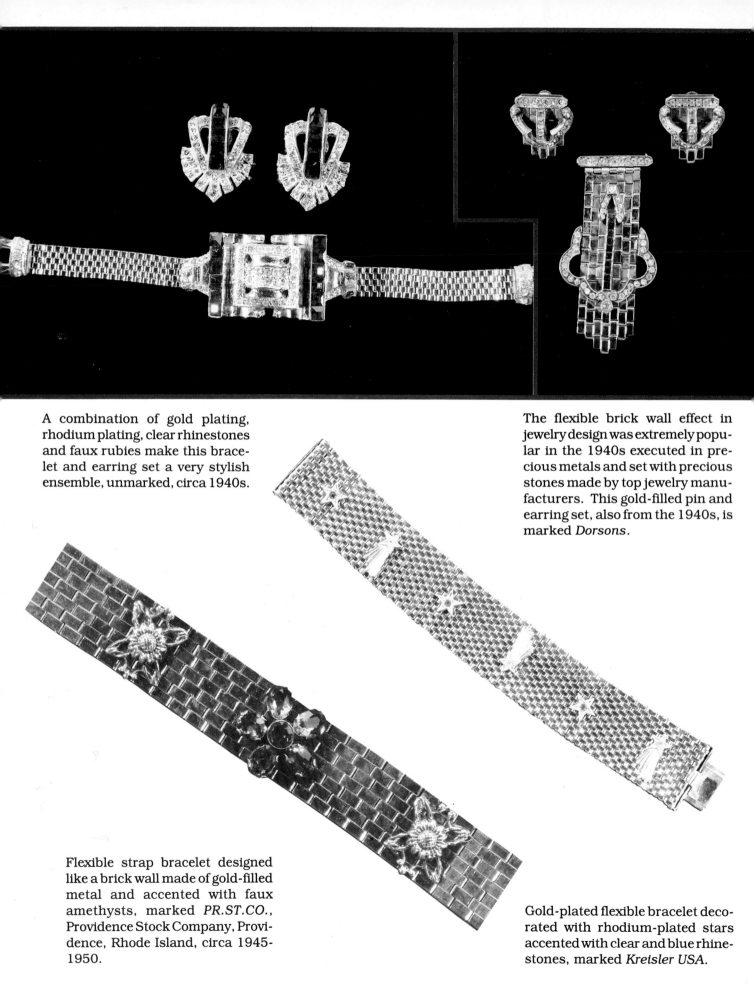

A combination of gold plating, rhodium plating, clear rhinestones and faux rubies make this bracelet and earring set a very stylish ensemble, unmarked, circa 1940s.

The flexible brick wall effect in jewelry design was extremely popular in the 1940s executed in precious metals and set with precious stones made by top jewelry manufacturers. This gold-filled pin and earring set, also from the 1940s, is marked *Dorsons*.

Flexible strap bracelet designed like a brick wall made of gold-filled metal and accented with faux amethysts, marked *PR.ST.CO.*, Providence Stock Company, Providence, Rhode Island, circa 1945-1950.

Gold-plated flexible bracelet decorated with rhodium-plated stars accented with clear and blue rhinestones, marked *Kreisler USA*.

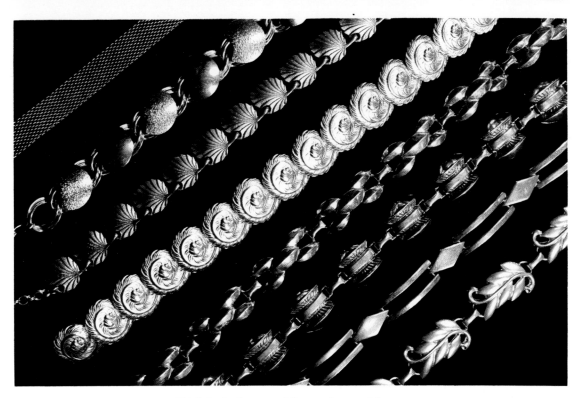

Eight choker necklaces in a wide variety of designs made of silvertone metal.

Pierced crescent-shaped disks bordered in rhinestones and further decorated with faux ruby baguettes form an elegant design for these gold-filled, screw-back earrings, Cohn & Rosenberger, circa 1940s.

Parure consisting of bracelet, brooch and earrings, gold- and rhodium-plated, rhinestone and pearl accents, marked *Dewees*.

Three floral brooches accompanied by original tags which read *Carl-Art Inc. of Providence, Rhode Island* (1943 to present.) The pins are marked *1/20-12kt Gold Filled on Silver,* 1940s.

A very unusual parure consisting of choker necklace, earrings and bracelet made of gold-plated metal set with green glass cabochon stones. The unique feature of this set is the bracelet which is also a watch (large center stone flips open) and a double locket (two smaller stones on each side of the watch flip open) which holds two pictures. The set is unmarked with the exception of the watch mechanism which is marked *Gotham.*

Flower brooch with petals rendered in gold-plated sterling silver, tipped with clear rhinestones and centered with large faux aquamarine marked *Leo Glass*. Leo Glass & Co.,Inc. was a New York manufacturer of costume jewelry from 1943 to 1957. Brooch made of gold-plated metal completely surrounded with clear rhinestone baguettes, unmarked, circa 1940s.

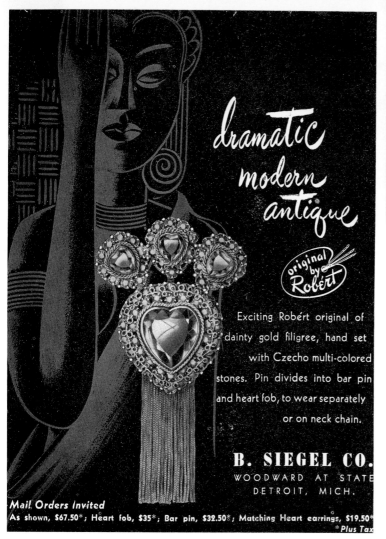

Jewelry by *Robért* advertised in
Vogue, November 1, 1946.

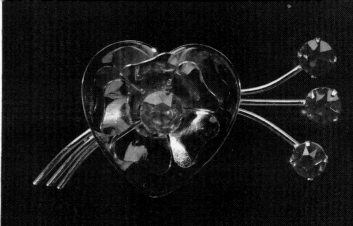

Flowers are blooming from this
heart-shaped brooch made of gold-
plated sterling silver and set with
colored glass stones marked Coro.

Brooch in the shape of a hat and a
cane made of gold-plated metal
and further decorated with green
glass stones, unmarked, circa
1940s.

Fur clip made of gold-plated brass
and set with faux emerald baguettes, circa 1935-1940.

Fashion Jewelry

In the 1940s, costume jewelry began to be sharply divided into two categories; fashion jewelry and novelty jewelry. Fashion jewelry was made by major manufacturers and designers such as Coro, Trifari, Mazer, Boucher, Haskell, Carnegie and many more. The list is endless because other manufacturers of costume jewelry followed the leads of the major producers. Fashion jewelry was cast out of better metals like sterling silver, for example.

Fashion jewelry, still considered a disposable commodity, was beginning to be designed to correlate with the latest fashion trends. The overall construction of the jewelry improved because a few European fine jewelry craftsmen who had worked for fine firms like Cartier and VanCleef & Arpels, fled to America during the war and found jobs with costume jewelry manufacturers like Boucher and Trifari. The jewelry was made along some of the same strict guidelines as that of fine jewelry. They shared their skills with top-of-the-line costume jewelry manufacturers and the quality and workmanship improved dramatically. Even though the jewelry was made to be worn for a short fashion season, its character and quality enabled it to be tucked away and saved in millions of American ladies' jewel boxes for many years.

Fashion jewelry manufacturers spent millions of dollars advertising their products in leading fashion magazines. It was sold throughout the country in major department stores and specialized boutiques. The department stores had designated counters for specific designer jewelry. It was a very competitive business at that time.

At times, fashion jewelry manufacturers, especially Trifari, chose to imitate the real jewelry made by firms like Cartier and Van Cleef. At other times, the jewelry was innovative in its design concept. Regardless of which form was chosen, there was plenty of supply and plenty of demand. Coro had three different lines of their costume jewelry which enabled almost everyone regardless of financial status to afford a piece of jewelry.

Opposite page:
A wonderful assortment of jeweled brooches pictured in the Spring and Summer Sears catalog of 1944. They were advertised as "Heirloom Quality" with classic designs made of gold-plated sterling silver and set with the finest simulated stones. Prices ranged from $13.50 (K) to $42.00 (D).

Hobé jewels advertised in *Vogue*, November 1, 1946.

Penguin Jewelry advertised for sale in 1946.

Rhinestone brooches popular in 1943 offered from Sears, Roebuck and Company.

The Clip-Pin above divides into smaller pin and two clips as shown in the small illustrations. Pins No. 11 and 1 are shown three-fourths actual size; others half actual size.

Duette (double-clip brooch) made of chromium-plated metal and set with clear rhinestones marked Patent Pending, circa 1938-1940.

Brooch made of rhodium-plated metal set with clear rhinestones and square (table cut) simulated sapphires.

Double brooch and matching earrings in original presentation box designed in the shapes of snowflakes made of gold-filled metal and set with red glass stones. This type of ornament was sometimes called a chatelaine pin because of the chains used to connect the two brooches. They were fashionable in the 1940s.

Merle Oberon, star of English and American films, wearing an Indian-inspired emerald necklace, *Life*, October 14, 1940.

Double sterling silver chatelaine pin attached by triple chains accompanied by matching earrings all set with blue glass stones in original presentation box, unmarked, circa 1940s.

Magnificent possessions!

pearls and diamonds . . . simulated of course
. . . for a future . . . feminine! Wear long
ropes of pearls . . . catch them dramatically
in a jeweled pin!

S. Bolasni

Hattie Carnegie

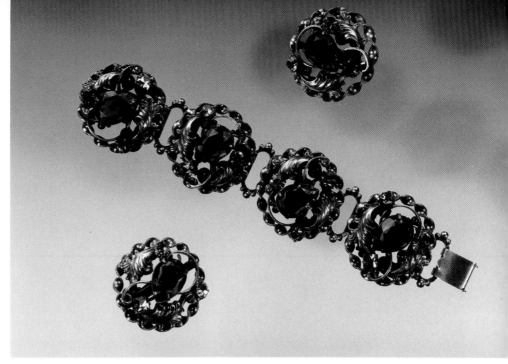

Links of twisted metal with feather motifs set with faux amethyst glass stones creates a stunning bracelet and earrings set that is, unfortunately, unmarked.

Opposite page, far left:
Hattie Carnegie pearl and rhinestone jewelry advertised in *Vogue* in November of 1946.

Opposite page, left:
Unusual brooch made with glass stones arranged into floral blossoms and attached to brass coils, marked *Vogue*, circa 1938-1940.

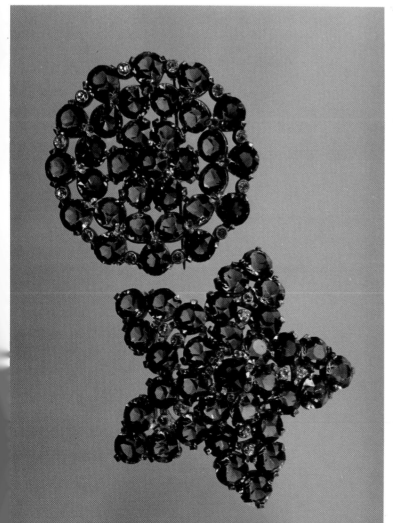

Large brooch made of white metal, set with Austrian crystal stones in various cuts, marked *Eisenberg Original*, circa 1935-1940.

The brilliance and clarity of the amethyst-colored Austrian crystals mounted in these two large white metal brooches is exceptional. Obviously made by the same maker, but unfortunately both are unmarked.

Another *McCall's* advertisement with Lana Turner in the M-G-M Picture "Slightly Dangerous," June, 1943.

Pewter-like brooch with leaf motif set with imitation pearl made by *Whiting & Davis*.

Trio of figural scatter pins with topaz-colored carved glass stones marked Sterling, circa 1940s.

"Retro" Silver and Single Stones

Glass stones from Austria, Czechoslovakia and Germany, once abundant, were now in short supply during the war years. Manufacturers used their own supplies sparingly but, once exhausted, had to resort to rations or underground purchases. Much of the jewelry of the previous decade was made with dozens of imported glass stones utilized in one piece of jewelry. The war, however, created a new retrospective classic look that is now often referred to as *Retro* jewelry. This look was created in fine jewelry as well as costume jewelry. In costume, for the sake of this book, the jewelry was made of sterling silver, sometimes with a heavy gold plating. The designs were sometimes big, massive, bold but yet stylized and elegant. The common theme would be a large rectangular faux gemstone. Aquamarines, amethysts, rubies and topaz stones were the most popular.

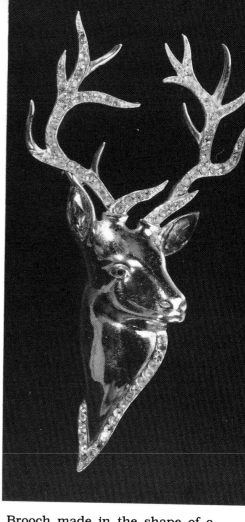

Brooch made in the shape of a deer cast in gold-plated sterling silver accented with clear rhinestones and marquise-shaped faux aquamarines, unmarked, circa 1940s.

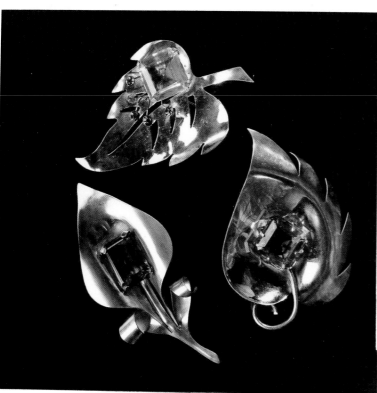

Three large brooches made in the shapes of leaves and set with single large glass stones, all unmarked, circa 1940s.

The scrolled base metal with large faux aquamarine makes this brooch extremely stylish.

This brooch in the shape of a three leaf clover with matching screw-back earrings is marked *Sterling*, circa 1940s.

French marcasite brooches and bracelets offered for sale in 1940 from W. H. Sims. Solid sterling silver mountings were used and prices ranged from $10.00 to $30.00 each.

Marcasite BROOCHES

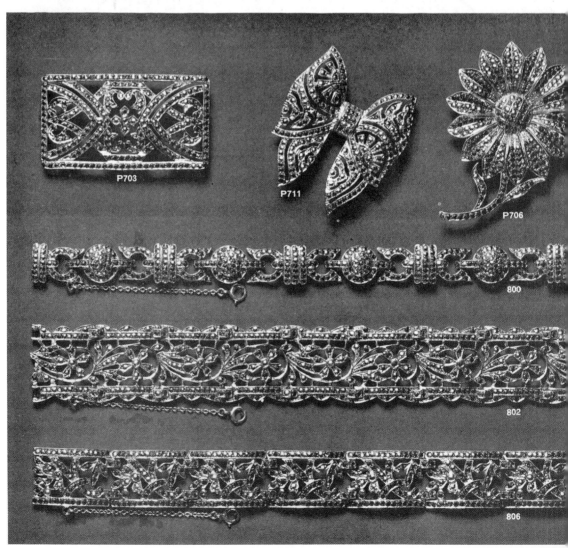

French marcasite bracelets and
brooches offered for sale from W.
H. Sims in 1940. Prices ranged
from $8.00 to $22.50 each.

Marcasite BRACELETS

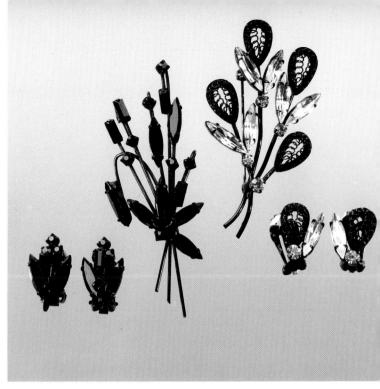

Two abstract floral pins with matching earrings made of japanned metal set with black and clear glass stones.

Two dynamic necklaces made of brass and glass.

Large amethyst-colored glass stones mounted in gold-colored metal makes this bracelet and earring set very appealing.

Jeweled bracelet by *Paul Flato* pictured in *Harper's Bazaar* in January, 1940. This bracelet is a typical example of the jewelry known today as Retro. Although this version is made of precious metal and genuine stones, costume jewelry manufacturers imitated this look in less expensive materials.

Scrolled metal bordering octagon-shaped pink glass stones makes this bracelet by *Coro* very eye catching. Bracelet made of gold over sterling silver (vermeil) with channel-set faux emeralds, marked *Coro*. Gold-filled link bracelet with alternating sections designed with leaf motifs and faux amethyst stones, unmarked, circa 1940s.

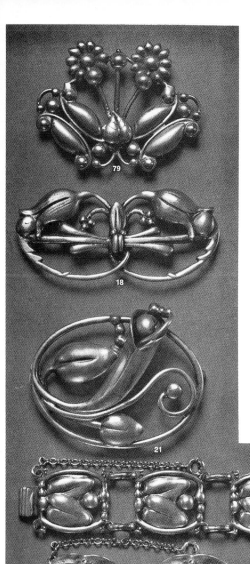

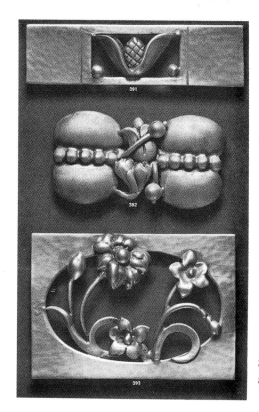

Sterling silver jewelry offered for sale from W. H. Sims in 1940.

Large tailored clip-on earrings, rhodium-plated and set with pink glass stones.

Silver-plated link chains were used
to create these stunning necklaces
and bracelet marked *Napier.*

Six pair of tailored earrings made
of rhodium-plated metal.

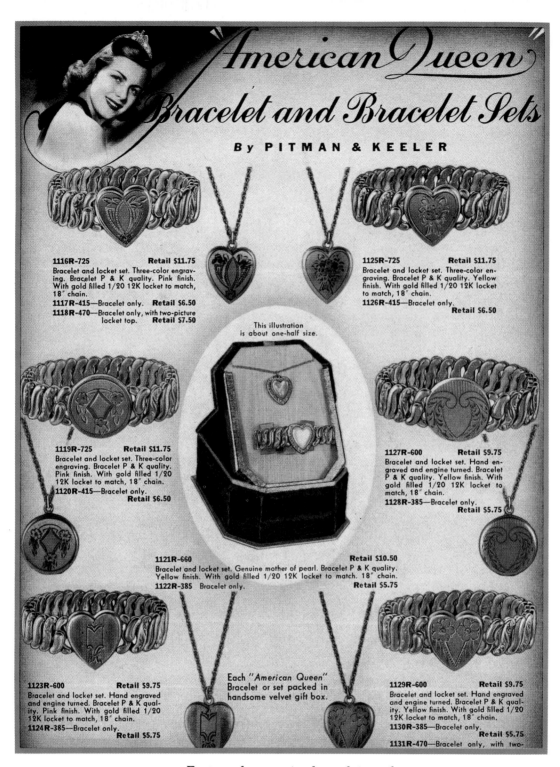

"American Queen"
Bracelet and Bracelet Sets

By PITMAN & KEELER

1116R-725   **Retail $11.75**
Bracelet and locket set. Three-color engraving. Bracelet P & K quality. Pink finish. With gold filled 1/20 12K locket to match, 18" chain.
1117R-415—Bracelet only. **Retail $6.50**
1118R-470—Bracelet only, with two-picture locket top. **Retail $7.50**

1125R-725   **Retail $11.75**
Bracelet and locket set. Three-color engraving. Bracelet P & K quality. Yellow finish. With gold filled 1/20 12K locket to match, 18" chain.
1126R-415—Bracelet only.
      Retail $6.50

This illustration is about one-half size.

1119R-725   **Retail $11.75**
Bracelet and locket set. Three-color engraving. Bracelet P & K quality. Pink finish. With gold filled 1/20 12K locket to match, 18" chain.
1120R-415—Bracelet only.
      Retail $6.50

1127R-600   **Retail $9.75**
Bracelet and locket set. Hand engraved and engine turned. Bracelet P & K quality. Yellow finish. With gold filled 1/20 12K locket to match, 18" chain.
1128R-385—Bracelet only.
      Retail $5.75

1121R-660   **Retail $10.50**
Bracelet and locket set. Genuine mother of pearl. Bracelet P & K quality. Yellow finish. With gold filled 1/20 12K locket to match. 18" chain.
1122R-385 Bracelet only.   **Retail $5.75**

1123R-600   **Retail $9.75**
Bracelet and locket set. Hand engraved and engine turned. Bracelet P & K quality. Pink finish. With gold filled 1/20 12K locket to match, 18" chain.
1124R-385—Bracelet only.
      Retail $5.75

Each "American Queen" Bracelet or set packed in handsome velvet gift box.

1129R-600   **Retail $9.75**
Bracelet and locket set. Hand engraved and engine turned. Bracelet P & K quality. Yellow finish. With gold filled 1/20 12K locket to match, 18" chain.
1130R-385—Bracelet only.
      Retail $5.75
1131R-470—Bracelet only, with two-

Engraved expansion bracelets and locket sets by *American Queen*. These popular designs were offered from Carson Pirie Scott.

Expansion bracelet made of yellow and pink gold-plated metal with engraved heart locket, marked *Lustern Made in USA.*

Flowers, Scrolls, Ribbons and Bows

Stylized flowers, scrolls, ribbons and bows were common motifs used in the designs. Jewelry was three-dimensional. Occasionally, there were variations to that theme but because of the lack of smaller glass stones from Europe, one large stone became the dominant characteristic of a design. Brooches, link and cuff bracelets, earrings, rings and necklaces were designed with a look that was classic, appealing and highly sought-after today. After the war, however, when the supply of rhinestones became plentiful again, the style of jewelry began to change and formed a closer link with the fashions of the times.

Three floral brooches decorated with hand-painting and set with rhinestones, marked *Coro*, circa 1940s.

Imported Czechoslovakian rhinestones set in pins, earrings and bracelets by *Royal Jewels of Pittsburgh* advertised in 1946.

Floral and leaf rhinestone pins by *Coro* advertised in *Seventeen* in December of 1947.

Daisy pin and earring set made of sterling silver with red glass stones. The necklace, also made of sterling silver, can be taken apart to form two identical bracelets.

Two floral brooches made of gold-plated sterling silver.

Lovely floral brooch made of gold-plated base metal and set with pavé rhinestones and clear and ruby-colored baguettes, circa 1940s.

This silver-plated basket brooch employs stamped, twisted, pleated and bent metal embellished with colored glass stones, unmarked, circa 1940s.

Gold-plated jewelry set with synthetic stones offered for sale in 1940. Prices in this grouping ranged from $7.50 to $28.50 each.

Circle brooch made of gold-plated metal set with clear rhinestones, marked *Trifari*. Fur clip cast in sterling silver with a gold wash and set with clear rhinestones, marked *CoroCraft*. Floral brooch made of gold-plated metal with rhinestone tipped petals, unmarked, circa 1940s.

Exceptionally large stylized floral brooch cast in silver with yellow and rose gold plating and set with amethyst-colored glass stones and clear rhinestone accents marked *Reinad*. The workmanship involved in creating this lovely retro brooch was clearly that done by a mastercraftsman.

Three stylized floral brooches, gold-plated and set with clear and colored rhinestones. The pin at the bottom right is marked *Mazer*, circa 1940s.

Floral brooch made of rhodium-plated base metal, clear and colored rhinestones with petals fashioned from amber-colored plastic.

Eisenberg Ice

HALLMARKED COSTUME PIECE ORIGINALS . . . IMPORTED STONES HAND-SET IN STERLING SILVER.

EISENBERG JEWELRY, INC. • MERCHANDISE MART, CHICAGO

Advertisement for *Eisenberg Ice* made of sterling silver and imported Austrian crystal stones, *Vogue*, September, 1947.

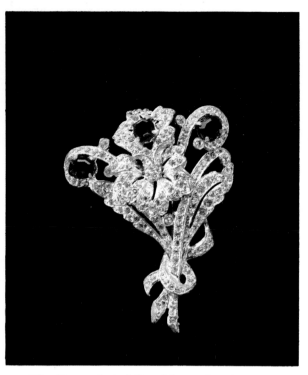

Rhodium-plated floral brooch set with clear rhinestones and faux rubies.

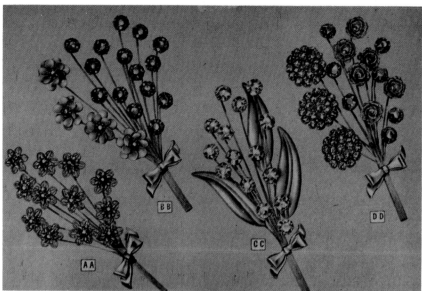

Sears advertised these brooches in 1944 as "Jewel-set Quiver Spray Pins" made of gold-plated sterling silver.

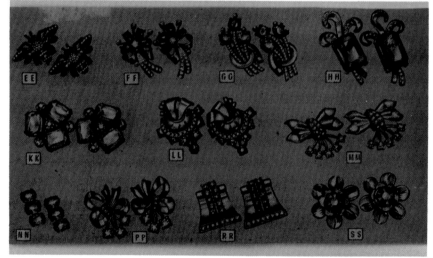

Gold-plated sterling silver earrings fashionable in 1944 featured in the Spring and Summer Sears catalog. Prices ranged from $2.18 (NN) to $15.00 (H H).

Brooch in the shape of a snowflake made of gold-plated metal and set with round and baguette rhinestones marked *Trifari*.

Sterling silver jewelry in the form of bracelets, brooches and earrings offered for sale in 1946 from the George T. Brodnax Company catalog. Prices ranged from $2.75 for the popular acorn motif earrings to $6.00 for the popular Calla Lily bracelet

Necklace designed with floral motif suspended from heavy link chain, marked *Sterling*, circa 1940s.

Flowers, Scrolls, Ribbons, and Bows 41

Three floral brooches cast in sterling silver, all unmarked, circa 1940s.

Large bow brooch made of base metal and set with large octagon-shaped, yellow glass stone.

Two sterling brooches designed with stylized floral motifs and set with faux amethyst and ruby glass stones.

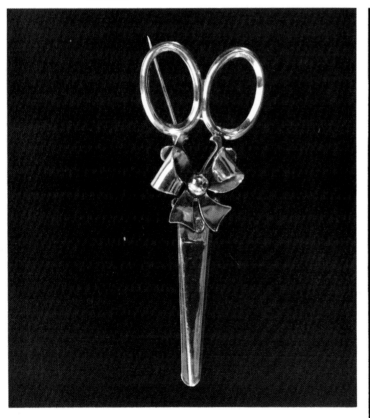

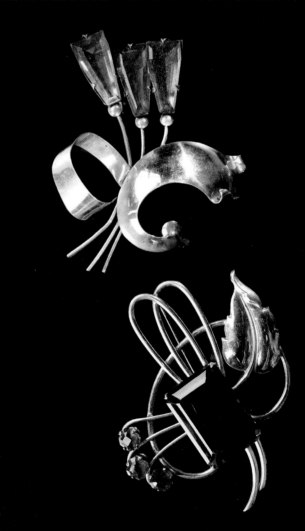

This brooch made in the shape of scissors accented with a bow is made of sterling silver.

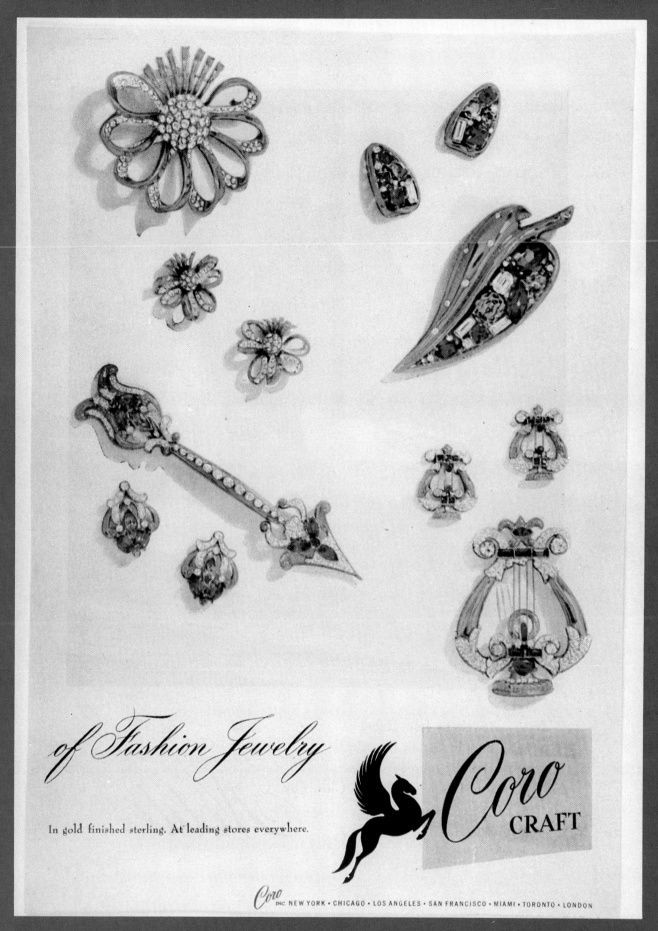

of *Fashion Jewelry*

In gold finished sterling. At leading stores everywhere.

CORO CRAFT

Coro INC. NEW YORK · CHICAGO · LOS ANGELES · SAN FRANCISCO · MIAMI · TORONTO · LONDON

More *CoroCraft* jewelry advertised in 1946.

Stylized floral spray made of sterling silver with square-cut, topaz-colored, glass stones and clear rhinestone accents. The two pairs of screw-back earrings are marked *Sterling*, circa 1940s.

Brooch made in the shape of a blossom rendered in gold-plated metal and set with clear rhinestones and faux aquamarines.

Obviously crafted by a fine jeweler, this large stylized floral brooch was cast in sterling silver, gold-plated and set with four different shapes of clear rhinestones, circa 1940s.

Goldtone metal is again used in this combination pendant/brooch on chain with matching earrings.

Stylized brooch cast in sterling silver with a gold plating and set with amethyst-colored glass stones and clear rhinestone accents marked *CoroCraft*, circa 1940s.

Two stylized floral brooches cast in sterling silver and set with glass stones, unmarked, circa 1940s.

This goldtone floral pendant with matching earrings, accented with clear and blue glass stones, came packaged in its original presentation box which reads *Jewelry of the Stars designed and created by Luis*. Inside the box was a warranty with the manufacturers' name *Plante & Fontaine Co. Inc., North Attleboro, Massachusetts*.

Stylized gold-plated brooch decorated the clear rhinestones, faux emeralds and simulated pearls, unmarked, circa 1940s.

Stylized brooch cast in sterling silver with gold plating and set with faux emeralds, unmarked, circa 1940s.

Rhodium-plated floral spray set with simulated sapphires and clear rhinestones, marked *Coro*.

Stylized brooch cast in sterling silver with a gold plating and set with simulated rubies accented with clear rhinestones, circa 1940s.

Stylized floral brooch and matching screw-back earrings made of gold-filled metal and set with green glass stones, packaged in original presentation box marked *Iskin*, Harry Iskin, Philadelphia, Pa., circa 1940s.

A collection of sparkling Coro Craft splendor...
Masterpieces
Fascinating jewels glowing with glamour..
design patented

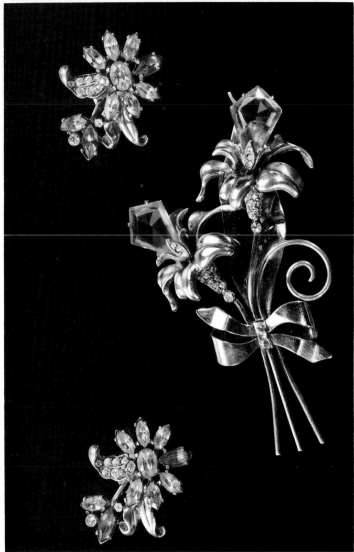

Stylized leaf, flower and bow designs were extremely common in the 1940s. These three examples were cast in sterling silver.

Stylized floral brooch cast in sterling silver and set with kite-shaped, simulated topaz stones. The floral earrings are made of base metal and also set with simulated topaz stones. Both pieces are unmarked but fine examples of the wonderful costume jewelry made in the 1940s.

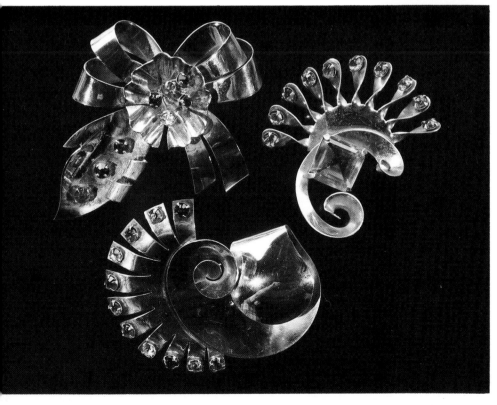

Three brooches made of sterling silver set with multi-colored glass stones, circa 1940s.

Model wearing simulated ruby and turquoise bow necklace pictured in *McCall's* in 1943.

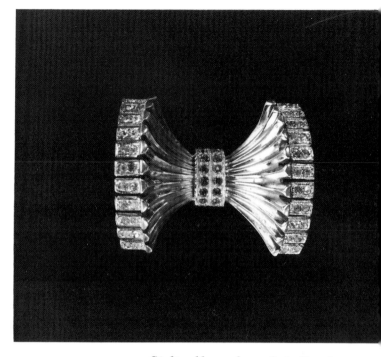

Stylized brooch made in the shape of a bow, cast in sterling silver and set with faux rubies, bordered with clear rhinestones, unmarked, circa 1940s.

Large stylized bow, rhodium-plated and set with simulated sapphires and clear rhinestones, marked *Trifari*.

Novelty Jewelry

Novelty jewelry, which was the other end of the costume jewelry spectrum, was usually stamped out of inexpensive base metals or made of molded plastics and sold in novelty stores. It was mass-produced, perhaps stamped out of inexpensive metals like brass and priced for a quick sale. Because of the lesser quality of the jewelry, not much was saved or treasured. Novelty jewelry had funny, fancy and whimsical subject matter which was derived from the times. Magazines of the period even provided do-it-yourself instructions for making novelty jewelry at home. Materials like leather, cork, fur, ceramic, buttons, beans and seeds were used to create inexpensive jewelry. In 1944, *McCalls' Needlework* magazine featured an ad for LUMI-NOUS jewelry that glowed in the dark. It was made with tropical sea shells from Cuba, Nassau, the West Indies and the Bahamas. Necklaces, hair ornaments, pins and earrings were offered for sale from the House of Gifts in Coral Gables, Florida. The prices ranged from $1.25 to $2.50.

Patriotic jewelry would also fall into the novelty jewelry category. It was extremely fashionable during the war with motifs such as flags, airplanes, Victory pins and military insignia. Wooden jewelry was another novelty favorite and animal themes were common made out of wood that was carved and sometimes set with glass eyes.

The Royal Pair
by Trifari

King-size and Queen-size Crowns, so exquisitely designed, so superbly crafted, they could be fashioned only by that royal house of jewelry art—Trifari.

Rhinestones, bright with all the fire of fabulous diamonds, and magnificently worked in Trifanium, lend coronation splendor to this royal pair of pins.

Housed in a royal box of pearl gray velvet, Trifari's crowns pay lavish Christmas tribute to Her Majesty, your Queen of Hearts. At quality stores everywhere.

The Pair of Pins, boxed . . . $17.50*

Jewels by **TRIFARI**

*Tax extra.

Gold-plated sterling silver brooches in spray and crown designs set with simulated pearls and multi-colored glass stones ranging in price from $7.25 to $36.00. This jewelry was offered from George T. Brodnax Company, Memphis, Tennessee.

Pin and earring set made of base metal fashioned like jeweled crowns and set with imitation glass stones.

A pair of crown pins by *Trifari* advertised in *Ladies' Home Journal*, December, 1948. Crowns and swords were two extremely popular jewelry motifs used in the 1940s.

EXCEPTIONAL VALUES IN STERLING SILVER JEWELRY. (Illustrations are exact size.)

You will find the attractive numbers shown here to be wonderful values at the prices asked. Each brooch is fitted with a dependable safety catch and all are substantially made. It would be difficult to find more attractive gifts at such reasonable prices.

47045 Sterling Silver Brooch, "High Horse" fitted with safety catch.........$1.50

47046 Sterling Silver Ear Rings, Rose design, match Brooch 47047......Pair 1.50

47047 Sterling Silver Spray Brooch, attractive Rose design, fitted with safety catch, matches Ear Rings 47046....................................$1.50
Set of Ear Rings and Brooch...................................... 3.00

47048 Sterling Silver Ear Rings, attractive Primrose design...........Pair 1.50

47049 Sterling Silver Brooch "Scottie," fitted with safety catch............. 1.50

47050 Sterling Silver Brooch, beautifully designed Horse, fitted with safety catch..$1.50

47051 Sterling Silver Ear Rings, attractive floral design, oxidized......Pair 1.50

47052 Sterling Silver Ear Rings, Four Leaf Clover....................Pair 1.50

47053 Sterling Silver Ear Rings, attractive floral design............Pair 1.50

47054 Sterling Silver Brooch, Prancing Horse, fitted with safety catch..... 1.50

47055 Sterling Silver Brooch, nicely designed "Airedale," fitted with safety catch..$1.50

47056 Sterling Silver Ear Rings, "Dutch Boy and Girl," (match brooch 47057)
....Pair $1.50

47057 Sterling Silver Brooch "Dancing Dutch Boys and Girls" fitted with safety catch (matches ear rings 47056)..............................$1.50
Set of Brooch and Ear Rings.....................................$3.00

47058 Sterling Silver Brooch, attractive Bow-Knot design, fitted with safety catch..$1.50

47059 Sterling Silver Brooch "Little Deer," fitted with safety catch........ 1.50

47060 Sterling Silver Sport Brooch, triple Horse Heads, fitted with safety catch 1.50

47061 Sterling Silver Spooner Pin, Four Leaf Clover design, fitted with safety catch..$1.50

47062 Sterling Silver Sport Brooch, fitted with safety catch................ 1.50

The prices quoted on this page include the 20% Federal Tax.

Sterling silver figural and floral
brooches popular in 1946.

Figural pins and screw-back earrings cast in sterling silver. The horseheads are marked *Lang*, the swordfish are marked *Beau*, circa 1940s.

Hand-made Hawaiian fish pins of sterling silver and enamel advertised for sale in 1946.

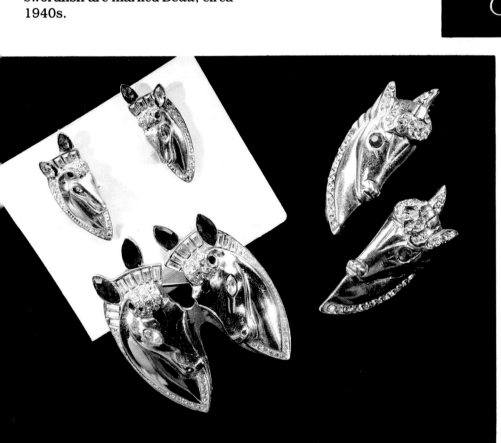

Pair of horsehead clips with matching earrings cast in sterling silver and set with rhinestones. The clips are attached to a mechanism known as a Coro Duette which connects and converts the clips into a brooch. The patent date on the mechanism is 1798867, circa 1930. The two horsehead pins on the right are made of plated base metal, unmarked.

Coin jewelry was very fashionable in the 1950s. Shown here are seven different earring examples in clip-on and screw-back styles.

A lovely pair of Victorian style slippers stamped in sterling silver marked *Lang*.

Pin and earring set made of sterling silver with lovebird motif in relief. Patent # 2,327,138, circa 1943.

Brooch and earrings in the shape of hands made of goldtone metal accented with imitation pearls, unmarked, circa 1950s.

Two brooches made of sterling silver designed in the shapes of hands, circa 1940s.

Two novelty brooches made of brass designed to resemble ladybugs and decorated with glass stones. The larger ladybug has a clear Lucite belly.

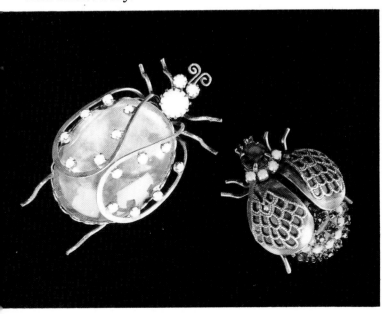

Peacock pin and earring set made of sterling silver. This set is unique in the fact that the feathers of the peacock are hinged to allow movement from the body of the bird. The pin is marked *Alex & Co. Sterling Siam*.

Brooches and earrings cast in sterling silver designed as swords and set with multi-colored glass stones. The brooch on the left is marked *Trifari*, circa 1940s.

Two gold-plated brooches, accented with colored glass stones and further ornamented with metal chains and tassels, both marked *Coro*.

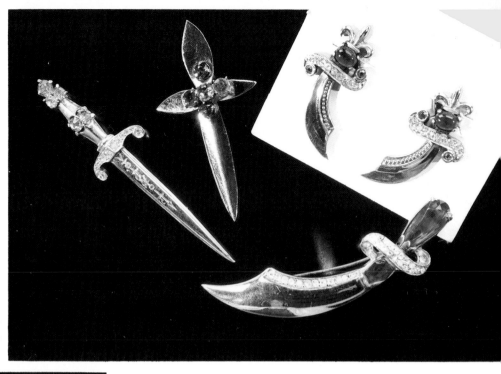

Chatelaine-type brooch designed as sheath and dagger cast in sterling silver, attached by a chain and decorated with enamel work and colored glass stones, unmarked.

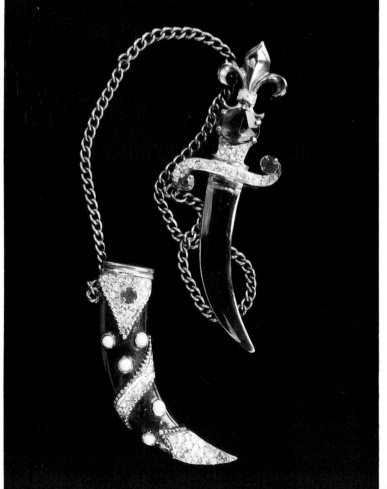

Figural brooch made of plated base metal and set with multi-colored glass stones, unmarked, circa 1940s.

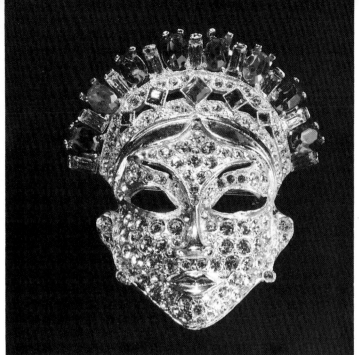

A new rendition of the Mazer mask, this time made into a brooch manufactured by Alex Carole, circa 1990.

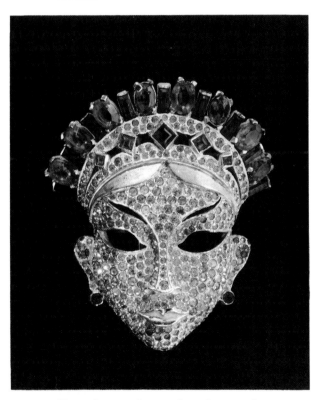

Fur clip made in the shape of a mask, rhodium-plated and set with clear rhinestones and crowned with faux sapphires, rubies and emeralds, marked *Mazer*, circa 1940s.

This winged knight, cast in sterling silver, gold-plated and decorated with black enamel and rhinestone accents, is marked *Reja*. Reja, Inc. was a New York manufacturer of costume jewelry from 1940 to the mid-fifties.

Someone did a lot of traveling in Europe to accumulate these great sterling silver charms for this bracelet.

Charm bracelets offered for sale in 1943 from Sears.

Wide segmented bracelet made of goldtone metal and decorated with simulated stones in a variety of shapes, colors and sizes.

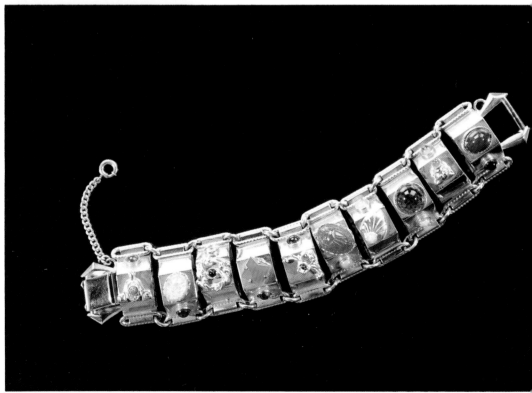

Forties Plastics

Experimentation in the field of plastics led to the perfection of clear Lucite which was used in the 1940s, especially by Trifari and Cohn & Rosenberger, in their manufacture of "jelly bellies." Although the term "jelly belly" is relatively new, the idea was a line of very detailed figural pins, mainly animals and marine life, made of sterling silver, some with a gold plating, and a clear Lucite belly. The Lucite was used to simulate rock crystal which had always been a favorite in jewelry design. Other designers and manufacturers made sterling silver figural brooches with a clear glass belly, while some used less expensive metal and colored plastic. Mexican designers also created animal pins made of silver with genuine stone-set bellies.

Bird of Paradise brooch cast in sterling silver with large clear faceted crystal belly and rhinestone accents. Unfortunately this piece is unmarked.

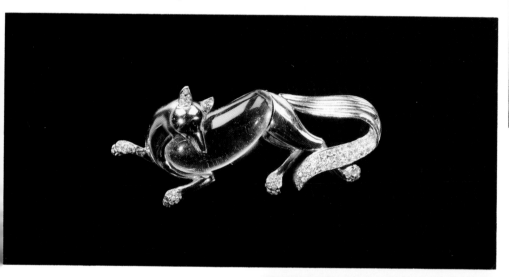

Brooch made in the shape of a fox cast in sterling silver with a gold plating and set with a clear Lucite belly commonly termed "jelly belly", marked *CoroCraft*, circa 1940s.

Necklace made of graduated Lucite cylinders capped with goldtone metal.

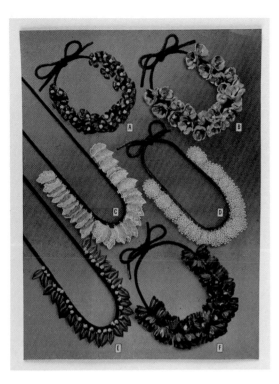

Flower necklaces, made to be worn full length, resembling a floral Hawaiian lei or tied shorter worn like a choker. Made of plastic, Sears offered them for sale in 1944 for $1.06 each.

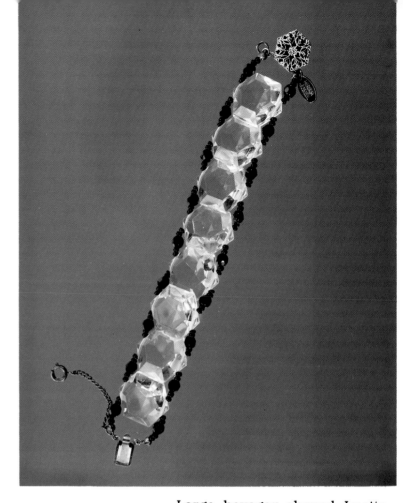

Large hexagon-shaped Lucite beads and black glass were used to create this bracelet marked *Miriam Haskell.*

The hand painting on these molded plastic flower earrings creates a delicate summertime look, circa 1940.

A common floral theme is evidenced here in these earrings made of glass, plastic and lacy gold-plated metal.

Dangle cluster earrings made of glass and plastic.

Brooch, necklace and bracelet made of sterling silver and dyed onyx with geometric motifs, all made in Mexico, circa 1940s.

Large brooch made of sterling silver designed in the shape of a bird perched on a limb, marked *Made in Mexico*.

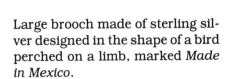

Mexican

Mexican jewelry became fashionable in America in the 1940s for a few reasons. First, there was an increased interest in cultural hand-made artisan jewelry. This interest was sparked in the 1930s with the work of Georg Jensen, the Danish silversmith. Secondly, since the preferred metal for costume jewelry during World War II was sterling silver, Mexican jewelry, as well as American Indian jewelry satisfied the need. Finally, good relations developed between the United States and the Latin American countries due to the "good neighbor" policy in the early 1940s and the taste for this cultural hand-made jewelry became more than just a whim with American tourists visiting the land south of the border.

A small mining community known as Taxco became the center of the jewelry industry in Mexico. An American architect known as William Spratling visited Mexico in 1925 to study Spanish Colonial architecture. By 1929, he settled in Taxco and made it his home. He revived the silversmithing trade by opening a shop selling regional Mexican crafts. By 1935, he began making silver jewelry. Tourism improved as roads opened and by 1946, Spratling alone had 422 workers. Hundreds of smaller workshops opened and silver jewelry with Spanish/Indian design became fashionable in America as well. Other prominent Mexican designers were the Castillo brothers, who worked in Spratlings' workshop, Antonio Pineda, Hector Aguilar and Salvador Terán.

Sterling silver figural brooch, carved amethyst face with large silver turban, marked *Silver J.P. Mexico 925*, circa 1940s.

Bracelet, screw-back earrings and ring made of sterling silver and set with cabochon-cut amethyst stones, marked *Sterling Mexico*, circa 1940s.

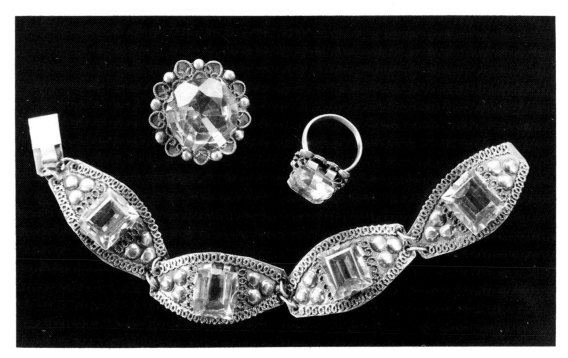

Segmented bracelet, pin and ring
made of silver and set with large
blue glass stones, marked *Mexico*,
circa 1940s.

Clusters of grapes form this necklace made of sterling silver marked
PLATA.

Extremely wide Peruvian silver link
bracelet marked *Welsch 900*, circa
1940s.

The New Look

In 1947, fashion designer Christian Dior managed to change the course of fashion history with his new spring collection called the "New Look". For years prior to this, fashion for women had retained its tailored, fitted, squared, utilitarian look. It was simple, fundamental clothing that was so very classic that one automatically associates that look with the 1940s. Partly responsible for this was Hollywood's Joan Crawford who personified that look, but war restrictions also affected the garment industry as well. Jewelry made during the war was designed to grab the attention of the saddened public and create an atmosphere of fantasy. The war-time jewelry often mimicked fine jewelry and it was hard to tell the real thing from a fake. The New Look fashions from 1947 on created a new atmosphere and by the time the 1950s rolled around, costume jewelry was appreciated for its own merit with its sparkle, glitz and fabulously fake look. The buying audience loved it.

La Tausca simulated pearls advertised in *Seventeen* in 1948.

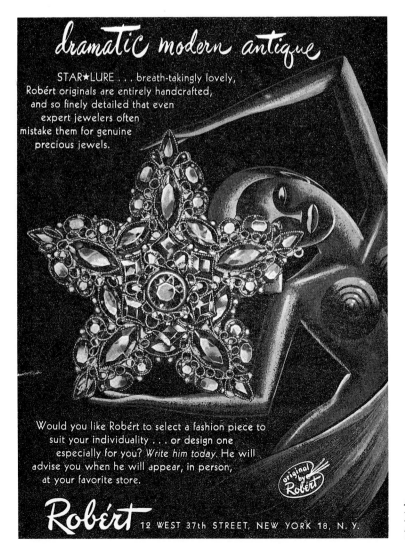

Advertisement for Originals by Robért pictured in Vogue in September, 1947.

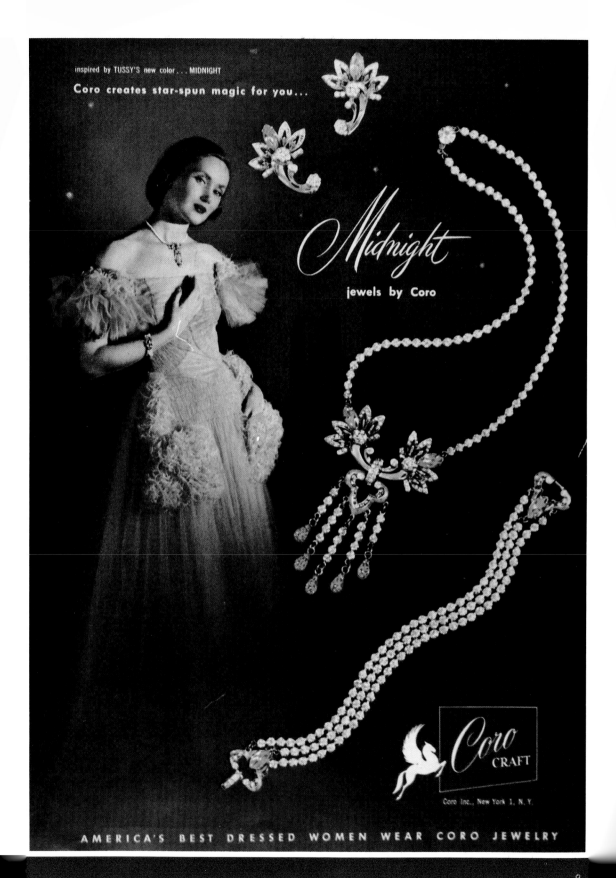

CoroCraft rhinestone jewelry advertised in *Vogue* in 1947.

Rhodium-plated sterling silver jewelry "Styled by Jo-Mar" in fashionable starburst pattern popular after World War II. This ad appeared
in *Vogue* in November of 1946.

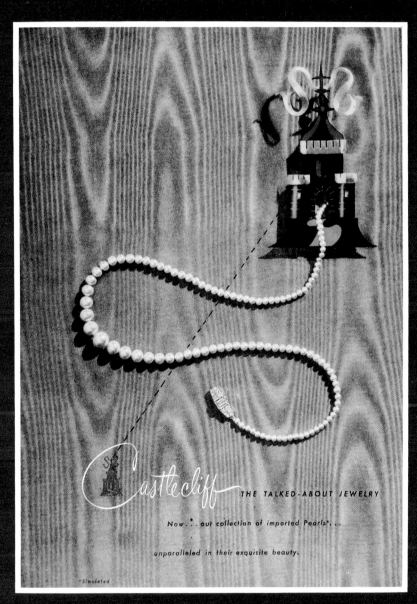

Ad for *Castlecliff* jewelry promot-
ing their collection of imported
simulated pearls, *Vogue*, September 1, 1947.

La Reine
by Coro

Coro
CRAFT

Necklace $6, bracelet $3, pin $3, earrings $2, necklace on model $12. Available in these pseudo gem colors: two-tone topaz, two-tone amethyst, ruby and white, all in gold-color settings. Two-tone light sapphire in silver-color setting. At all leading stores, or write Coro Inc., N. Y. 1

A M E R I C A ' S   B E S T   D R E S S E D   W O M E N   W E A R   C O R O   J E W E L R Y

Furs by Gunther Jaeckel

© 1955 Coro Inc., Design Pat. Pend.

Matched sets by *Coro* called "La Reine" made of goldtone and silvertone metal and set with simulated colored glass stones, *Vogue*, 1955.

Part Two - The Fifties

Glitzy jewelry stands out most in people's minds when they think of the jewelry made and worn during the 1950s. When Marilyn Monroe sang "Diamonds are a girls best friend", women went crazy trying to emulate that diamond look and rhinestones fit the bill. The Austrian crystal company Swarovski and others in Eastern Europe supplied a tremendous amount of stones to American manufacturers and designers. Extravagant parures consisting of necklaces, bracelets and earrings were made in multitudes at that time. Major manufacturers made complete sets offered in many different colors packaged in satin and velvet presentation boxes. Copy-cat companies presented similar styles and prices varied accordingly. Some sets were made of sterling silver and others were made of base metals but almost all of the sets were rhodium-plated. They were advertised as non-tarnishing. Some were even plated with gold and set with rhinestones. Necklace and earring sets were popular as well as pin and earring sets mounted with clear and colored rhinestones. Manufacturers like Trifari, Coro, Eisenberg, Mazer, Schreiner, Boucher, Weiss and more produced tremendous amounts of glitzy fashion jewelry during the 1950s. Since these companies had made such an impression on the buying public in the 1940s, it was easy for them to continue their trend of producing fine designs in the 1950s. Other new manufacturers and designers emerged to create similar styles and satisfy the tastes of the times.

Two pendants turned so foiled stones and their mounts are visible.

Beautiful Gold Filled Costume Jewelry

More gold-filled pendant-necklace and earring sets popular in 1950.

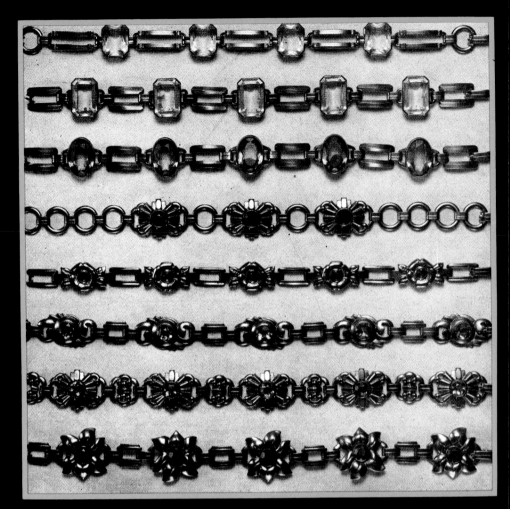

Gold-filled bracelet sets available in 1950 from H.M. Manheim Company catalog. They were offered with either genuine, synthetic or simulated stones in classic Retro designs.

Seven colored glass and crystal beaded bracelets with decorative and jeweled clasps, unmarked, circa 1950s.

Rhodium-plated clip-on earrings in large tailored designs. The earrings on the top left are marked *Bartek*, circa 1950s.

Button-style clip-on earrings were fashionable in the 1950s.

Sterling silver jewelry by *Danecraft* advertised in *Vogue* in 1955.

Rhinestone and pearl jewelry by *Coro* offered in the 1954 Sears Christmas Book.

Brooch representing a tree with multi-colored, marquise-shaped stones (navette) and smaller rhinestone accents, marked *Joseph Wiesner N.Y.*, circa 1950s.

Rhinestone jewelry by *Taylor Maid* of Philadelphia, advertised in *Vogue* in 1955.

Frosted emerald glass is transformed into this lovely leaf brooch decorated with clear rhinestones marked *Jomaz*.

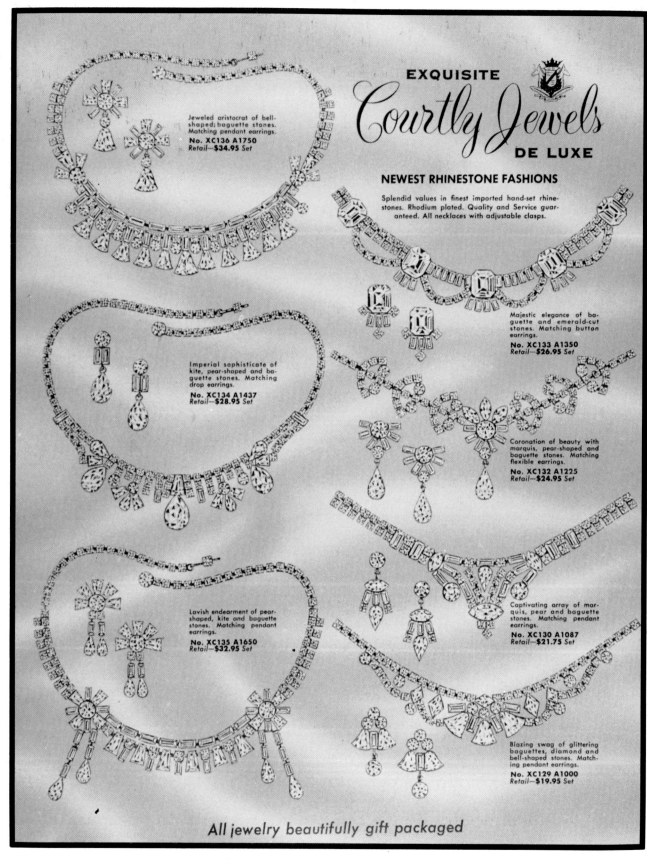

EXQUISITE
Courtly Jewels
DE LUXE

NEWEST RHINESTONE FASHIONS

Splendid values in finest imported hand-set rhinestones. Rhodium plated. Quality and Service guaranteed. All necklaces with adjustable clasps.

Jeweled aristocrat of bell-shaped; baguette stones. Matching pendant earrings.
No. XC136 A1750
Retail—$34.95 Set

Imperial sophisticate of kite, pear-shaped and baguette stones. Matching drop earrings.
No. XC134 A1437
Retail—$28.95 Set

Lavish endearment of pear-shaped, kite and baguette stones. Matching pendant earrings.
No. XC135 A1650
Retail—$32.95 Set

Majestic elegance of baguette and emerald-cut stones. Matching button earrings.
No. XC133 A1350
Retail—$26.95 Set

Coronation of beauty with marquis, pear-shaped and baguette stones. Matching flexible earrings.
No. XC132 A1225
Retail—$24.95 Set

Captivating array of marquis, pear and baguette stones. Matching pendant earrings.
No. XC130 A1087
Retail—$21.75 Set

Blazing swag of glittering baguettes, diamond and bell-shaped stones. Matching pendant earrings.
No. XC129 A1000
Retail—$19.95 Set

All jewelry beautifully gift packaged

Rhodium-plated hand-set rhinestone necklace and earring sets by *Courtley Jewels* offered for sale in 1954.

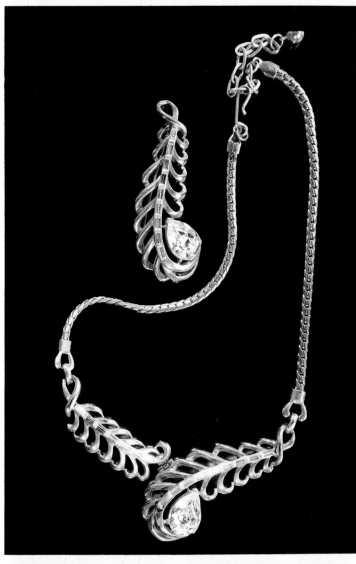

Necklace and brooch fashioned like feathers made of plated base metal and set with large teardrop rhinestones and accented with rows of baguette rhinestones, unmarked, circa 1950s.

The "Regency" necklace and earring set by *Coro*, popular in 1958, was offered for sale by Block Wholesale Company. The retail price for this set was $36.00.

This gold-plated necklace with rows of glittering baguettes was called *The Regency Necklace* made by *CoroCraft* in 1958.

Stylized necklace and earring set of gold electroplated metal and clear rhinestones, marked *Mazer Bros*, circa 1950s.

The exceptional quality of this parure by *Weiss* is largely due to the brilliance of the Austrian crystals that were used in this three piece set.

Necklace and matching bracelet made of goldtone metal and alternating rhinestones, unmarked, circa 1950s.

Necklace, earrings and matching brooch made of clear rhinestones, marked *CATHE*.

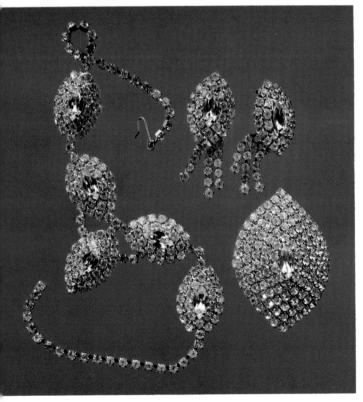

DELUXE RHINESTONE
JEWELRY FASHIONS
BY
Courtly Jewels

Extraordinary Values in Finest Imported Diamond - Faceted Rhinestones for Maximum Brilliance! All Stones Hand-Set! Non-Tarnishable Rhodium-Plated . . . Lifetime Guaranteed for Wear and Luster. Handsomely Gift Boxed.

A Fancy Floral Spray Necklace of finest navette and baguette stones. Distinctive chain treatment . . dainty rhinestones encircle baguettes! Matching floral drop earrings
No. C/10
Retail .... **$24.95** Set

B Elegantly entwining necklace of brilliant baguette and round stones. Matching button earrings
No. C/9
Retail .... **$22.50** Set

C Heirloom necklace elaborately fashioned of octagon, square-cut and round stones to treasure forever. Matching pendant earrings
No. C/8
Retail .... **$18.95** Set

D A dramatic array of rhinestones accent square-cut drop. Matching earrings
No. C/3
Retail .... **$7.95** Set

E Graceful garland necklace of navette and round stones. Matching pendant earrings. Available in ice blue with crystal (as shown) or all crystal.
No. C/6
Retail .... **$14.25** Set
Same as above, in all crystal.
No. C/6R

F "Sincerely yours" sweetheart necklace a'glow with octagon, navette and round stones. Matching drop earrings.
No. C/5
Retail .... **$12.95** Set

G A glorious garland of flashing rhinestones! Matching pendulum earrings
No. C/4
Retail .... **$9.95** Set

H Artfully draped rhinestones spark navette - center stone. Matching lobe - shaped earrings. Available in ice blue (as shown) or crystal.
No. C/2
Retail .... **$6.95** Set
Same as above, in crystal.
No. C/2R

J Flashing pear-shaped stones sparked with circles of rhinestones. Matching drop earrings
No. C/7
Retail .... **$16.95** Set

K Sparkling beauty of graduated round stones ending in center drop. Matching earrings
No. C/1
Retail .... **$5.95** Set

Rhodium-plated rhinestone jewelry by *Courtly Jewels* popular in 1957.

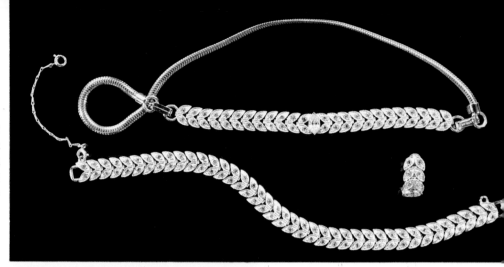

Parure consisting of flexible choker necklace, bracelet and screw-back earrings, cast in sterling silver with a rhodium plate, and set with clear rhinestones, circa 1950. Courtesy of Marie Rodino.

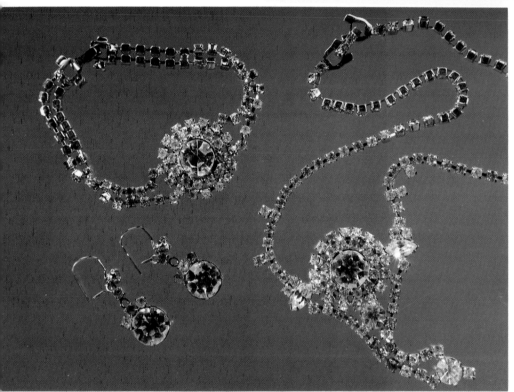

Parure consisting of necklace, bracelet and earrings made of rhodium-plated metal set with clear rhinestones, unmarked. The earrings were originally of the screw-back variety and later changed for pierced ears.

Choker necklace, bracelet and screw-back earrings, silvertone metal set with rows of gray pearls and rhinestone rosettes. The earrings were on the original card that reads *Donna Costume Jewelry*.

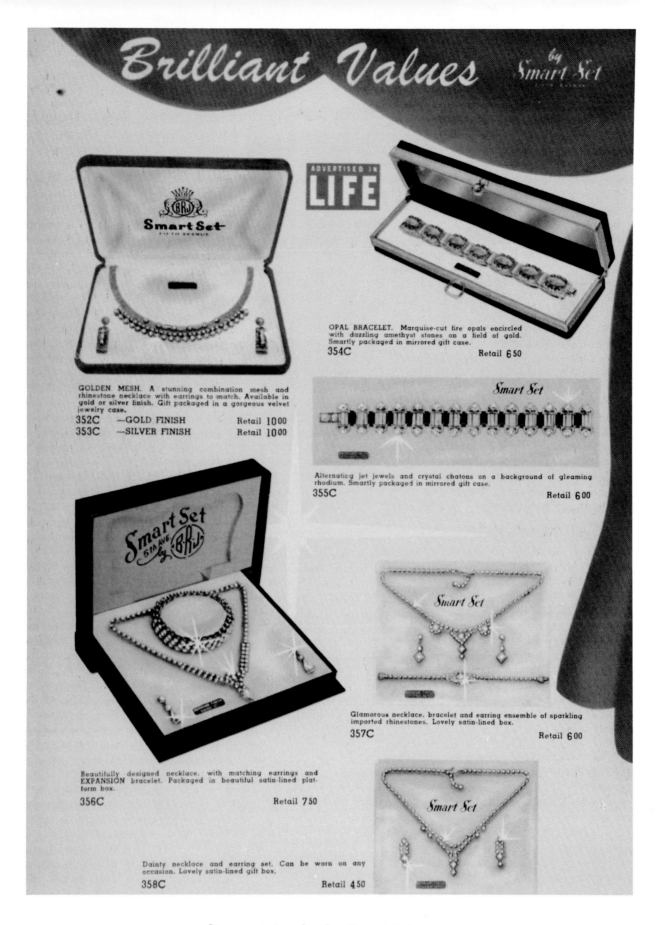

Brilliant Values

by Smart Set

ADVERTISED IN LIFE

OPAL BRACELET. Marquise-cut fire opals encircled with dazzling amethyst stones on a field of gold. Smartly packaged in mirrored gift case.

354C   Retail 6 50

GOLDEN MESH. A stunning combination mesh and rhinestone necklace with earrings to match. Available in gold or silver finish. Gift packaged in a gorgeous velvet jewelry case.

352C —GOLD FINISH   Retail 10 00
353C —SILVER FINISH   Retail 10 00

Alternating jet jewels and crystal chatons on a background of gleaming rhodium. Smartly packaged in mirrored gift case.

355C   Retail 6 00

Glamorous necklace, bracelet and earring ensemble of sparkling imported rhinestones. Lovely satin-lined box.

357C   Retail 6 00

Beautifully designed necklace, with matching earrings and **EXPANSION** bracelet. Packaged in beautiful satin-lined platform box.

356C   Retail 7 50

Dainty necklace and earring set. Can be worn on any occasion. Lovely satin-lined gift box.

358C   Retail 4 50

Stone-set jewelry by *Smart Set*, Fifth Ave, New York, offered for sale in 1957.

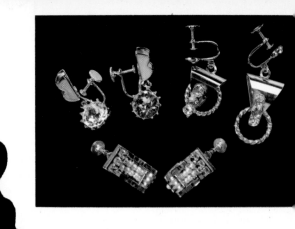

Jewels

by

TRIFARI ®

Screw-back and clip-on earrings, gold-plated and set with clear rhinestones, unmarked, circa 1950s.

Opposite page
Left:
"Vanity Fair" rhinestone jewelry by *Trifari* advertised in the *Social Spectator* in January of 1957.

Bottom left, inset:
Rhinestone expansion bracelet with rectangular section which opens to reveal photo made by *Carl Art*.

Top right, inset:
Small tailored earrings made of gold-plated metal and set with clear rhinestones and imitation seed pearls.

Oversized goldtone earrings in floral, leaf and abstract designs enhanced with clear rhinestones, circa 1950s.

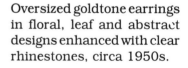

Earrings made of goldtone metal accented with clear rhinestones.

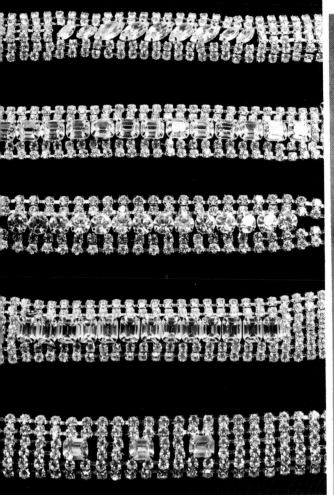

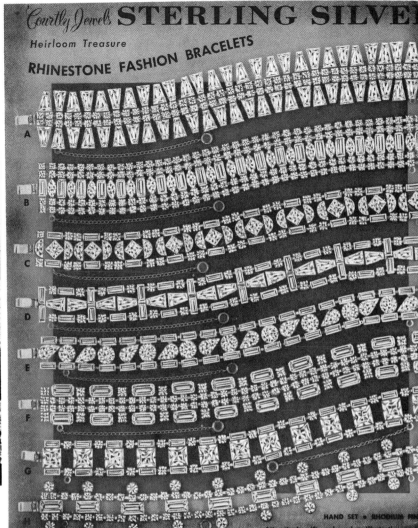

Five rhinestone bracelets from the 1950s, all unmarked.

Rhodium finished sterling silver rhinestone bracelets by *Courtly Jewels* featured in the 1954 Spors catalog. The bracelets were given specific names such as *Moonglow*, *Monte Carlo*, *Star of Paris*, and *Vendome*. Prices ranged from $19.50 (H) to $37.50 (A).

Molded pink glass leaves and alternating stone-set links form this attractive braclelet from the 1950s.

Bands of gold-plated metal separate short links set with clear rhinestones to form this bracelet marked *Jomaz*. Bracelet made of gold-plated metal formed with links of floral rosettes set with cushion-cut faux emeralds and clear rhinestones and hand-painted trim, unmarked.

Brooch and matching earrings made of goldtone metal set with clear rhinestones, unmarked, circa 1950s.

Advertisement for *Eisenberg Ice* pictured in *Vogue* in 1955.

Clear rhinestones are mounted in unique earring settings fashioned from goldtone metal.

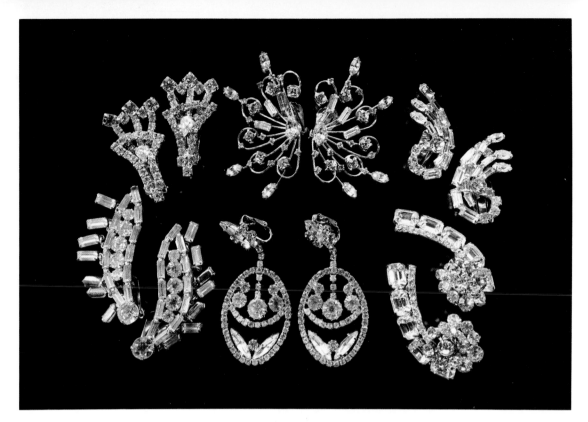

Six fine examples of clip earrings made of rhodium-plated metal and set with clear rhinestones designed for evening wear.

Chaton, baguette, navette, teardrop, rectangular and octagon-shaped clear rhinestones were used in these rhodium-plated examples from the 1950s.

Atomic

After the war, jewelry designed with starburst or sunburst patterns became known as "atomic" around 1945. This jewelry resembled firework displays or explosions or the popular design of an atom with circling particles and the trend continued well into the 1950s. Particularly fashionable in brooch and earring sets, these "atomic" ornaments were sometimes three dimensional with large stones placed in the center and pieces of metal with smaller stones radiating from the center point. Other variations to that same theme include jewelry designed with snowflake patterns dripping in rhinestones.

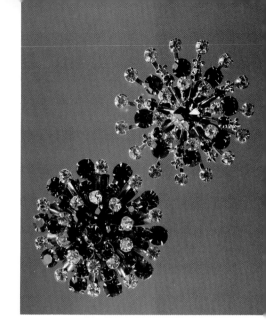

Clear and smoky gray rhinestones were used to create these two brooches with snowflake and starburst motifs.

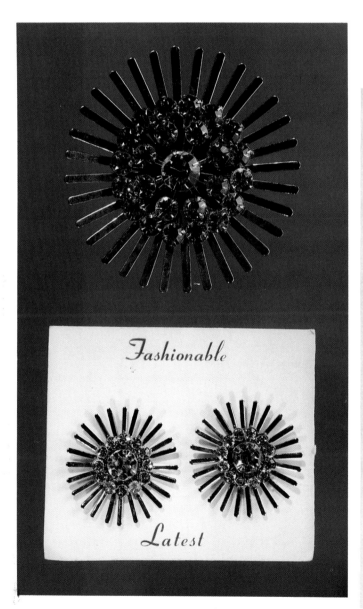

Sunburst pin and earring set made of goldtone metal and clear rhinestones.

Gold-plated jewelry by *Castlecliff* popular in 1955.

Atomic 85

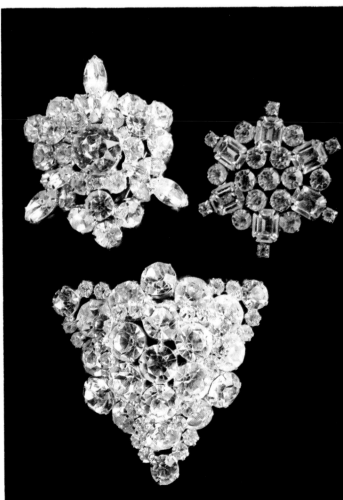

Pin and earring set made of blue rhinestones, marked *Judy Lee*.

Three brooches using the starburst and floral motifs popular in the late forties and early fifties made of silvertone metal and set with clear, pink and smoky gray rhinestones, all unmarked.

Four unmarked rhinestone pins set with multi-colored glass stones.

Three brooches set with clear rhinestones. The snowflake brooch on the top right is marked *Weiss*.

Parture consisting of necklace, earrings and brooch made of japanned metal and set with blue and green glass stones. Original tag reads *Jewelry by King.*

Five brooches set with smoky gray rhinestones designed in the atomic style which was popular after World War II.

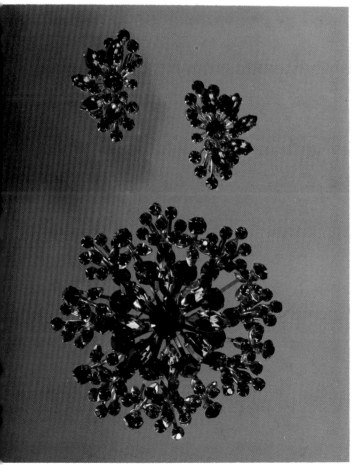

The atomic-style jewelry so popular after World War II is evident in this pin and earring set made of chartreuse rhinestones.

The six fabulous designs for these brooches were created with silver-colored and rhodium-plated metal and smoky gray rhinestones. The brooches on the top right and bottom left are marked *BSK*.

Pin and earring set made of black crystals formed into clusters, marked *Laguna*. Pin and earring set with black glass stones mounted in japanned metal, unmarked.

Three large rhinestone brooches from the 1950s, all unmarked.

Smoky Gray

Clear and smoky gray rhinestones were commonly used. Albert Weiss popularized the smoky gray rhinestone and called it the "Black Diamond."

Clip earrings made with smoky gray, clear and iridescent rhinestones.

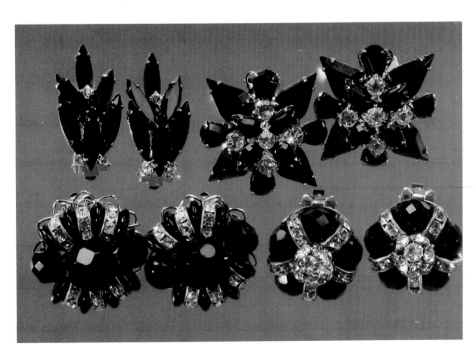

The beauty of French jet (black glass) enhanced by clear rhinestones is captured here in these clip earrings from the 1950s.

Matched set consisting of necklace, bracelet and clip earrings
made of faux topaz stones, unmarked, circa 1950s.

Seven necklaces of black and clear
rhinestones set in rhodium-plated
metal designed for evening wear in
the 1950s by *Weiss*.

Necklace made of triangular-
shaped smoky topaz glass stones,
unmarked, circa 1950s.

Various cuts of smoky gray rhinestones were used to create this pin and earring set marked *Pell*. Pell was founded in 1941 in New York by the Gaita brothers.

A stunning group of black and smoky gray rhinestone bracelet and earring sets from the 1950s.

Light and dark blue glass stones in various shapes were used to create this floral pin and earring set and diamond-shaped brooch from the 1950s.

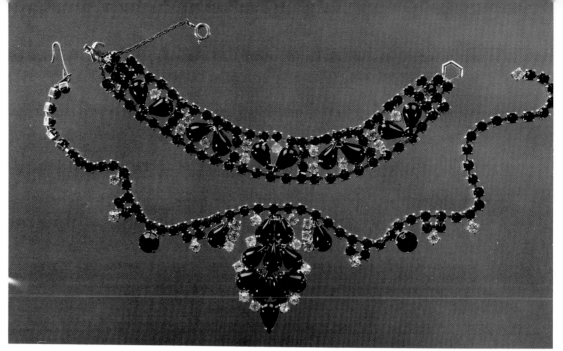

Black and clear rhinestones used in combination form this stunning necklace and bracelet set, circa 1950s.

Four pairs of earrings made with clear and smoky gray rhinestones.

Two bracelet and earring sets of citrine-colored glass stones accented with smoky gray and topaz-colored rhinestones, unmarked, circa 1950s.

Matched set consisting of necklace, bracelet and clip-on earrings
made of silvertone metal with clusters of smoky gray glass beads and
imitation pearls. The set, which
was never worn, is accompanied
by its original tags which read
Lucien Creation.

Matched set consisting of adjustable necklace, bracelet and earrings made with simulated smoky
topaz stones made by Albert Weiss.

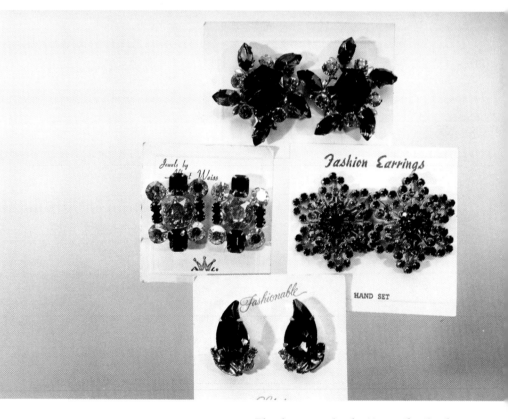

The bigger, the better - that's the
common theme in this group of
fashion earrings from the 1950s.

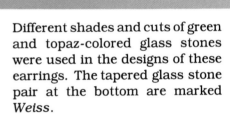

Different shades and cuts of green and topaz-colored glass stones were used in the designs of these earrings. The tapered glass stone pair at the bottom are marked *Weiss*.

Two elegant examples of topaz-colored rhinestone earrings worn for evening wear in the 1950s. The pair on the left is a screw-back that dangles while the pair on the right is a clip-on that climbs up the ear.

Four variations of the same theme clearly observed in these hand-set rhinestone fashion clip-on earrings from the 1950s.

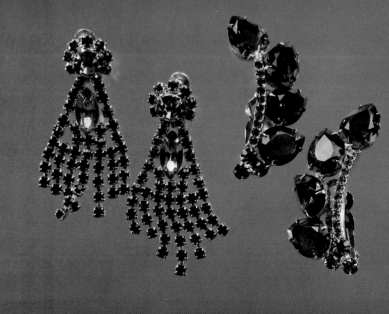

Aurora Borealis

In 1953, technicians at the Swarovski company of Austria perfected the iridescent "Aurora Borealis" crystal which took the jewelry scene by storm. Also responsible for its success was fashion designer Christian Dior who utilized this stone in the early 1950s. Necklaces, earrings, bracelets and brooches were set with this brilliant and colorful stone. In addition, ropes of crystal iridescent beads, either single strands or multi-strands, became fashionable.

Two pin and earrings sets from the 1950s.

Clip earrings set with iridescent glass stones.

Pin and earring set made with smoky gray rhinestones and aurora borealis crystals, unmarked.

Four dazzling rhodium-plated necklaces set with blue and aurora borealis rhinestones accented with clear rhinestones and imitation pearls.

Pin and earring set made of silvertone metal and set with red and iridescent glass stones, unmarked, circa 1950s.

Dynamic three piece parure made of goldtone metal and set with aurora borealis Austrian crystals marked *Bellini*. Courtesy of Marlene Franchetti.

Floral brooch with matching earclips made of base metal and set with multi-colored glass stones, marked *Schreiner New York*.

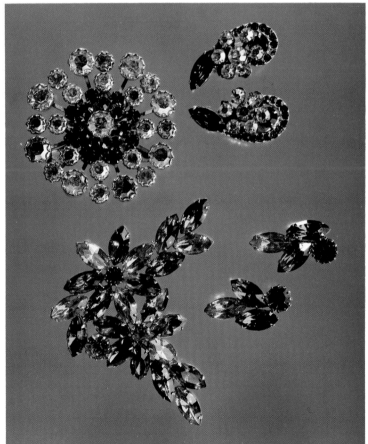

Two more examples of the popular rhinestone pin and earring sets from the 1950s.

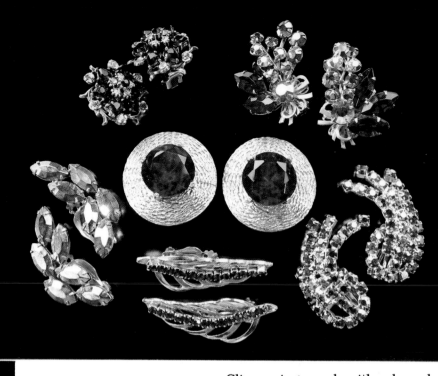

Clip earrings made with ruby red, garnet and iridescent glass stones.

Brooch and earring set made with rows of iridescent glass stones, marked *Kramer*.

Necklace and bracelet set, goldtone metal with openwork design set with iridescent glass cabochons, marked *Coro*.

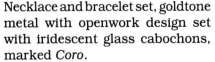

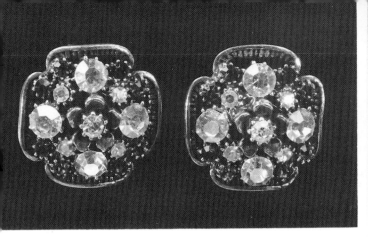

Fashion stone-set earrings by *Florenza*.

Lovely floral brooch, gold-plated and set with pink and iridescent glass stones, marked *Regency Jewels*. Courtesy of Marlene Franchetti.

Two necklaces of the same design made of goldtone and silvertone metal and set with glass stones. The original tag reads *Wolcott*, circa 1950s.

Clip earrings made with iridescent beads, glass stones and pearls, unmarked, circa 1950s.

Center right:
Pin and earring set, rhodium-plated and set with clear and iridescent glass stones.

Wonderful iridescent stones mounted in japanned metal make these earrings quite illuminating.

Bracelet and matching earrings of light blue glass stones accented with aurora borealis rhinestones, unmarked.

Necklace and matching earrings made of gold-colored metal and set with octagon-shaped, mirror-backed, glass stones marked *Florenza*.

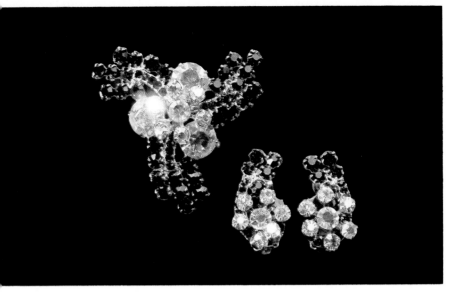

Pin and earrings made of plated base metal and set with green and iridescent glass stones, unmarked, circa 1950s.

Pin and earring set made of plated base metal and set with green and iridescent glass stones, unmarked, circa 1950s.

Clear and aurora borealis rhinestones were used to create these glittery earring examples from the 1950s.

Brooch made of goldtone metal and set with purple and iridescent glass stones, marked *Karu*. Screwback earrings marked *Lisner*.

Beaded necklace and matching earrings accented with goldtone metal and aurora borealis rhinestones, unmarked, circa 1950s.

Necklace and matching bracelet designed with one row of emerald-colored rhinestones bordered with two rows of aurora borealis rhinestones mounted in rhodium-plated metal.

Six bracelets made of goldtone and silvertone metal and set with glass stones, all unmarked, circa 1950s.

Three bracelets with matching earrings, tailored in design, made of goldtone and silvertone metal and set with colored glass stones, unmarked, circa 1950s.

A lovely group of bracelets and matching earrings set with translucent glass stones bordered with aurora borealis rhinestones, circa 1950s.

Oversized multi-faceted glass stones, set with aurora borealis rhinestones mounted in silvertone and goldtone metal, form these tailored bracelets with matching earrings. Again, unmarked, but of exceptional quality.

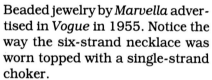

Beaded jewelry by *Marvella* advertised in *Vogue* in 1955. Notice the way the six-strand necklace was worn topped with a single-strand choker.

Screw-back and clip-on earrings made with different varieties of Venetian and Bohemian glass.

Triple strand of glass beads with matching earrings (two different designs) marked *Japan*, circa 1950s.

Beads

Multi-strand necklace and matching earrings made of red and orange glass beads, marked *Western Germany*.

A model wearing a glass beaded necklace featured in a German fashion magazine in 1958.

Spiral bracelets and matching earrings made of glass beads, marked *Germany*.

This Austrian crystal double strand necklace with matching earrings is further enhanced by the use of a few raspberry-like beads, circa 1950s. Courtesy of Marie Rodino.

Beautiful matched set consisting of necklace, bracelet and two pairs of earrings made of emerald-colored Austrian crystal beads, marked *DeMario*.

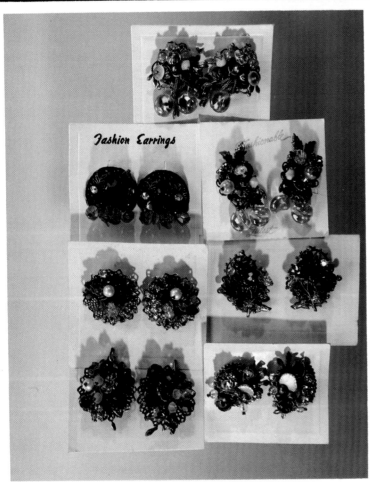

Antiqued brass settings, rhinestones, glass beads and pearls were used in combination in the designs of these earrings from the 1950s.

Expansion bracelets made with clear or icy blue rhinestones offered for sale in 1957.

Expansion bracelet and matching cluster earrings made with sapphire-colored and aurora borealis Austrian crystals.

Expansion bracelet and matching cluster earrings made with clear Austrian crystals.

Bracelet and earring set made of Venetian beads (Aventurine), amber-colored glass beads and rondelles.

Necklace composed of sapphire-colored glass beads embellished with silver-colored metal filigree. The floral motif in the center is further adorned with clear rhinestones.

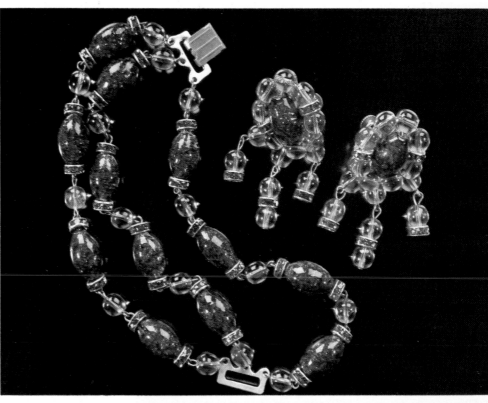

Spiral bracelet composed of five strands of amber, green and iridescent glass stones with matching cluster clip-on earrings, unmarked, circa 1950s.

Glass beads and rhinestone rondelles create this attractive necklace and earring set from the 1950s.

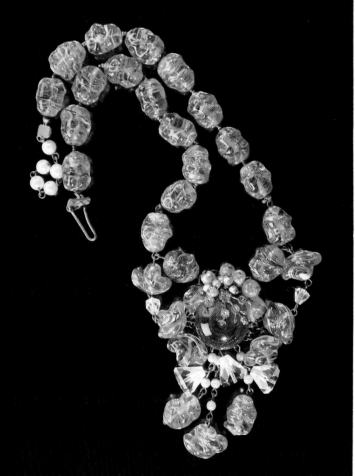

Necklace made of Bohemian glass beads accented with clear crystals and imitation pearls.

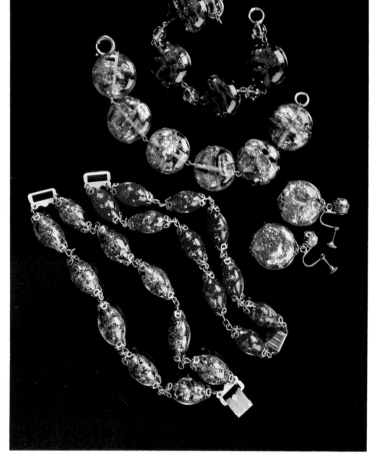

Handmade bracelets and earrings made of Venetian glass from the 1950s.

Unusual combination of Venetian beads, baroque pearls, Austrian crystal and rhinestone rondelles form this necklace and matching earrings set.

Parure consisting of necklace, bracelet and earrings made of lavender and amethyst-colored crystals, simulated pearls, rhinestones and brass, unmarked, circa 1950s.

Seven pair of clip earrings made of Austrian crystal, pearls and rhinestones.

Fashion model wearing a red, white and blue beaded necklace, circa 1957.

An Indian-inspired demi-parure made with simulated glass rubies and sapphires suspended from rhodium-plated rhinestone settings, unmarked, circa 1950s.

Three spiral bracelets made of multi-colored glass stones.

Spiral bracelet and matching earrings made of Austrian crystal beads and rhinestone rondelles, circa 1950s.

Multi-strand necklaces with matching earrings made with glass beads, marked *Western Germany*.

Matched set consisting of necklace, brooch and earrings resembling grape clusters, *Jewelry by King,* circa 1960.

Glass beads and rhinestones in shades of blue and green make up this lovely bracelet and earring set by *Juliana*.

Outstanding four-strand Austrian crystal bracelet and matching cluster earrings, marked *DeMario*. Necklace and matching bracelet also made of Austrian crystal, unmarked, circa 1950s.

Square glass beads and clear crystal spacers form these bracelet and earring sets from the late 1950s.

Festoon-style necklace with matching earrings fashioned from lavender and pink glass stones.

Two gold-colored choker necklaces set with large triangular-shaped glass stones and smaller rhinestone accents.

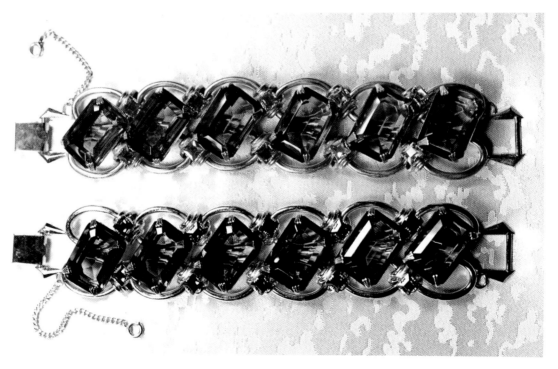

Two oversized link bracelets, one set with faux topaz stones in goldtone metal and the other set with faux sapphire stones in silvertone metal, unmarked, circa 1950s.

Faceted stones

A dramatic effect was achieved in the manufacture of this parure composed of pear-shaped, square, rectangular and chaton-cut Austrian crystal stones in shades of blue and green. Unfortunately, this set is unmarked.

Two matched sets consisting of rhodium-plated link necklaces and bracelets set with purple and green glass stones. The original tag reads *Jewels by Schauer Fifth Ave*.

Faux sapphires were used to create this group of earrings from the 1950s. Center left pair is marked *Bogoff*; center right pair is marked *Weiss*; bottom center pair is marked *Pastelli*.

Different shades and cuts of green glass stones were used to create these clip-on and screw-back earrings from the 1950s.

Rhodium-plated necklace and matching dangle earrings set with faux sapphires and emeralds, unmarked, circa 1950s.

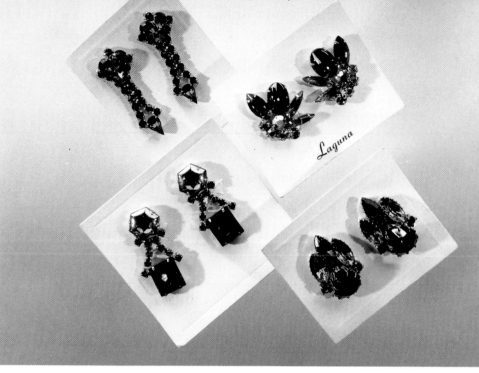

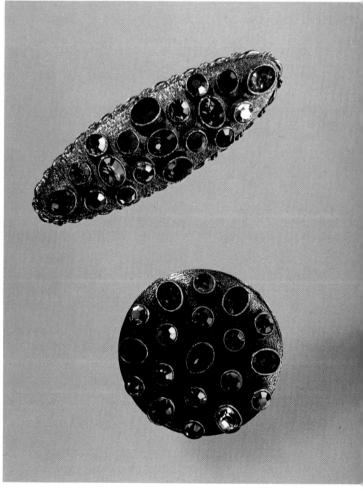

Two brooches made of chased gold-colored metal and set with multi-colored glass stones marked *ART*.

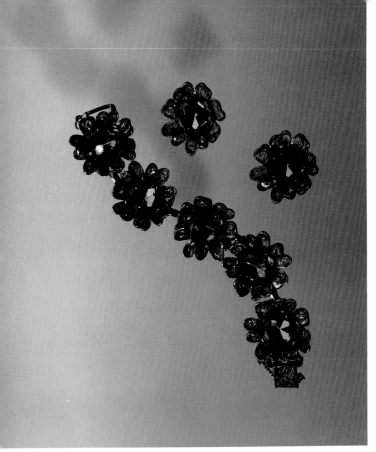

Bracelet and earrings made of pot metal and set with large mirror-backed glass stones, which produce color changes when viewed from different angles, marked *Judy Lee*.

Round brooch made of gold-colored metal and set with amethyst and fuchsia colored glass stones marked *Weiss*. Rectangular brooch composed of pink and fuchsia glass stones marked *Austria*.

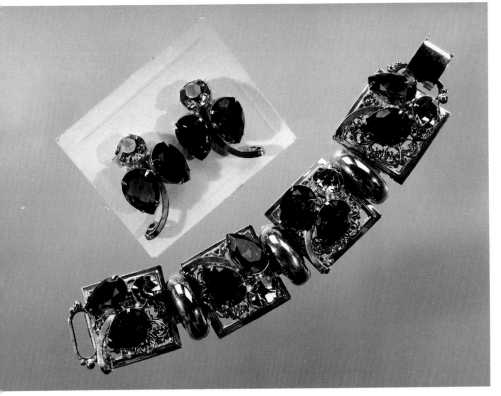

Bracelet and earring set, goldtone metal in four openwork segments, embellished with purple glass stones, unmarked, circa 1950s.

Three necklaces made of amber-
and topaz-colored glass stones, all
unmarked, circa 1950s.

Large brooch made in the shape of
a butterfly executed in base metal
and set with octagon-shaped, topaz-colored stones and smaller
rhinestone accents.

Clip earrings made of topaz- and
citrine-colored rhinestones, all
unmarked, circa 1950s.

Double pin and earring set, scroll design, rhodium-plated metal with clear rhinestones bordering faux emeralds and sapphires mounted in a checkerboard pattern, marked *Boucher*. This set was a wedding present to Marie Rodino in September of 1950.

Butterfly brooch made of base metal and set with various shades of green glass stones, unmarked. Turtle brooch made of japanned (blackened) base metal and set with blue, green and iridescent glass stones, unmarked, circa 1950s.

Two stylized brooches set with pink glass rhinestones.

Floral pin and earring set made of silvertone metal and blue glass stones, unmarked, circa 1950s.

Parure consisting of necklace, bracelet and earrings made of gold-plated metal and set with simulated topaz stones, unmarked, circa 1950s.

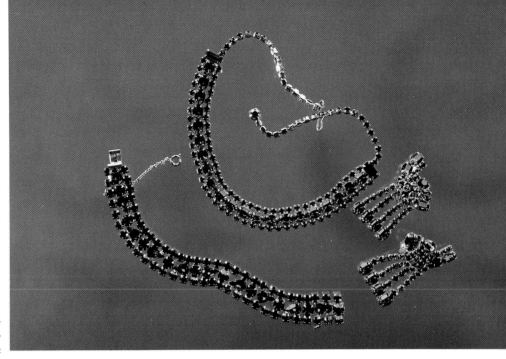

Three stylish bracelets set with round and pear-shaped glass stones in goldtone and silvertone metal, unmarked, circa 1950s.

Five elegant brooches made of gold-plated metal and set with pink and multi-colored glass stones, unmarked, circa 1950s.

Designed with large rectangular faux amethysts bordered with smaller lavender rhinestones, this necklace and bracelet set by an unknown manufacturer is quite appealing.

Four link necklaces set with large glass stones by *Schauer of Fifth Ave.*

Three exquisite brooches in gold- and rhodium-plated floral settings mounted with clear rhinestones and large faux amethyst, sapphire and topaz glass center stones, unmarked.

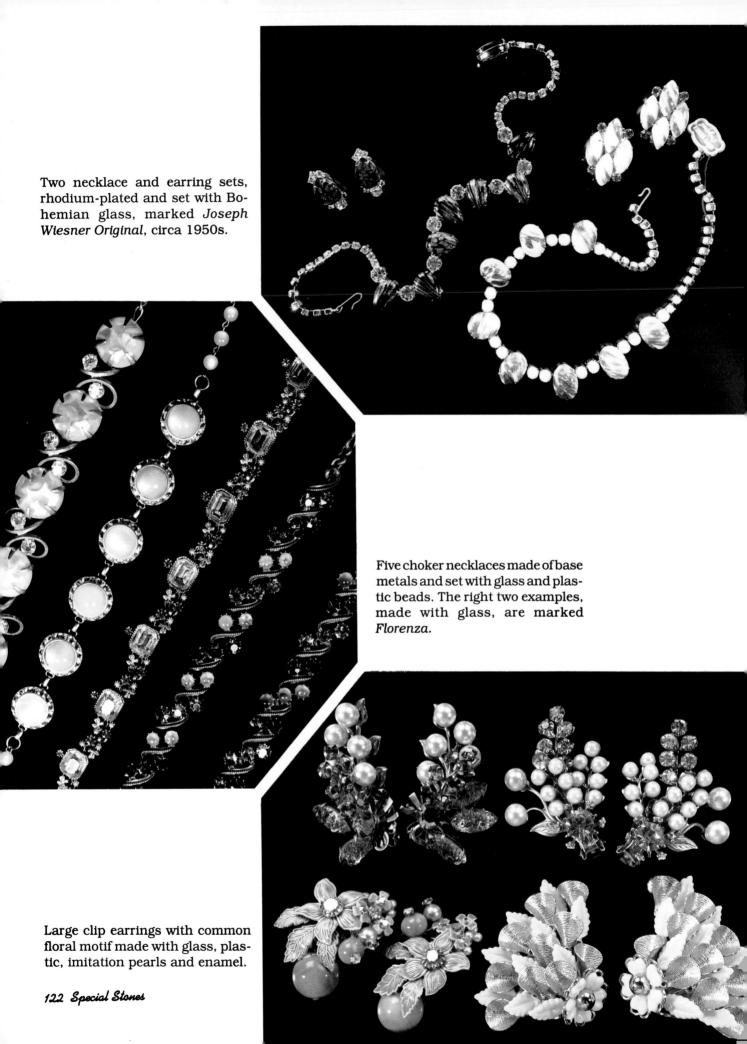

Two necklace and earring sets, rhodium-plated and set with Bohemian glass, marked *Joseph Wiesner Original*, circa 1950s.

Five choker necklaces made of base metals and set with glass and plastic beads. The right two examples, made with glass, are marked *Florenza*.

Large clip earrings with common floral motif made with glass, plastic, imitation pearls and enamel.

Special Stones

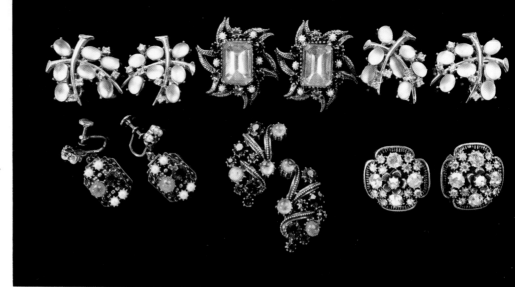

Six pairs of stone-set fashion earrings, marked *Florenza*.

Necklace and two brooches set with opaque orange glass stones.

Rectangular links of silvertone metal serve to frame the individual blocks of red and blue confetti Lucite mounted in these two bracelet and earring sets from the 1950s.

Necklace, bracelet and earring set made of goldtone metal with prong-set pink glass stones, unmarked, circa 1950s.

Unusual effects were achieved with the use of marbleized glass stones set in these necklaces, bracelets and earrings from the 1950s.

Clip-on earrings designed with floral motifs created by the use of odd-shaped glass stones, beads, pearls and gold-plated metal.

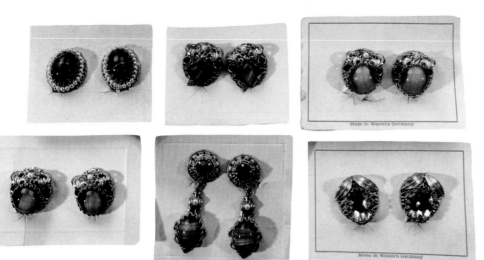

Gold-plated metal, glass, pearls and enamel were utilized to create these fine examples of earrings made in Western Germany.

Goldplated bracelet and matching earrings decorated with floral designs and set with small iridescent rhinestones and large pink glass cabochon stones, marked *HAR*. The same style earring is also pictured in silverplated metal with blue glass stones.

A combination of transparent, translucent and opaque glass stones were used to create these elegant bracelets that were designed for evening wear in the 1950s.

Three bracelets set with opaque blue glass stones.

Four lovely bracelets made with glass stones and beads, all unmarked, circa 1950s. (Don't pass up a great piece of jewelry just because it is not marked. It could very well be a designer piece that originally only had a paper tag or label.)

Earrings made of goldtone metal and set with translucent yellow glass stones.

Pin and earring set made of goldtone metal set with opalescent and pink glass stones, unmarked.

Clip earrings, rhodium-plated and set with transparent and opaque blue glass stones. The earrings on the top right were made by Albert Weiss.

Below:
Six link bracelets mounted with colored glass stones, imitation pearls and mother of pearl, unmarked, circa 1950s

Five bracelets made of goldtone and silvertone metal set with glass, plastic and simulated pearls. The bracelet in the center is marked *Hollycraft.*

Large cabochon glass stones bordered in smaller pink rhinestones form this unusual unmarked necklace and bracelet set. Brooch is set with rectangular cabochon glass stones and smaller aurora borealis rhinestones in openwork setting.

Three bracelets accompanied by matching earrings made of goldtone and silvertone metal and set with colored glass stones.

Opaque glass stones in shades of lavender and blue were utilized to create these three bracelets from the 1950s.

Metalwork

In the 1950s, gold-plated tailored jewelry was again in vogue made with a polished or textured finish. Rhodium-and silver-plated designs were popular as well as jewelry made of sterling silver and copper. Although the designs were basically flat, not three dimensional, they appealed to the 1950s career oriented or working woman. Simple designs for day were popular and more elaborate pieces were used for evening wear. Choker necklaces, bangle and charm bracelets, earrings and brooches were designed with this tailored look. The two most popular manufacturers of this type of jewelry were Monet and Napier.

Sterling link bracelet and matching earrings ornately designed with silver bead ornamentation, marked *Napier*.

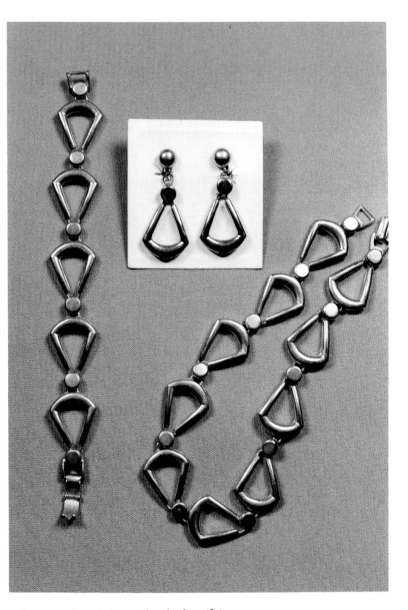

Designed as triangular links, this necklace, bracelet and earrings set from the 1950s is unmarked.

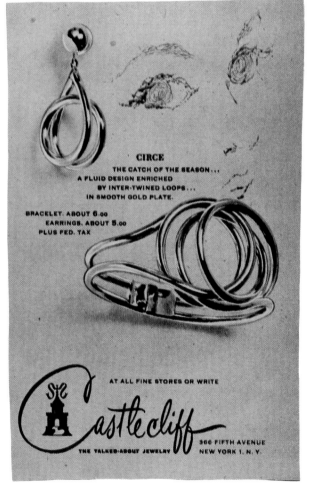

Gold-plated jewelry by *Castlecliff* advertised in 1953.

Four goldtone choker necklaces designed with abstract motifs, unmarked, circa 1950s.

More oversized earrings made of goldtone metal and set with pearls and rhinestones.

Clip earrings in three tailored designs made of rhodium-plated metal, unmarked, circa 1950s.

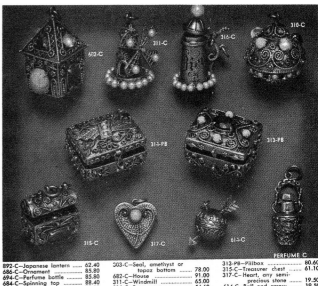

892-C—Japanese lantern 62.40	303-C—Seal, amethyst or topaz bottom 78.00	313-PB—Pillbox 80.60
686-C—Ornament 85.80	682-C—House 91.00	315-C—Treasurer chest 61.10
694-C—Perfume bottle 85.80	311-C—Windmill 65.00	317-C—Heart, any semi- precious stone 19.50
684-C—Spinning top 88.40	316-C—Beer mug 54.60	614-C—Ball and arrow....... 19.50
306-C—Pocketbook, opens 72.80	310-C—Ornament 80.60	Perfume-C—Top opens 28.60
308-C—Pitcher, agate center 49.40	314-PB—Pillbox 78.00	309-C—Bucket 91.00
693-C—Wishing well 67.60		

Very detailed Victorian reproduction charms offered for sale in 1957 from the Jack Kellmer Company catalog.

Chatelaine pin, charm bracelet and matching earrings made in the Victorian revival style by *Coro*.

Charm bracelet featuring The Ten Commandments, marked *Coro*, circa 1957.

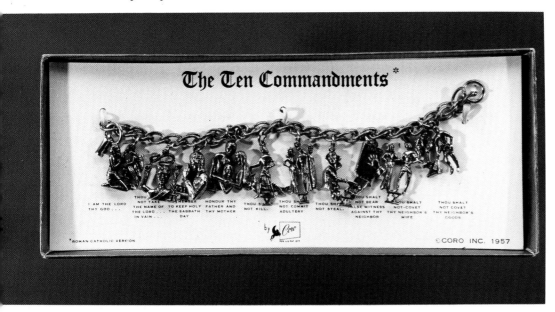

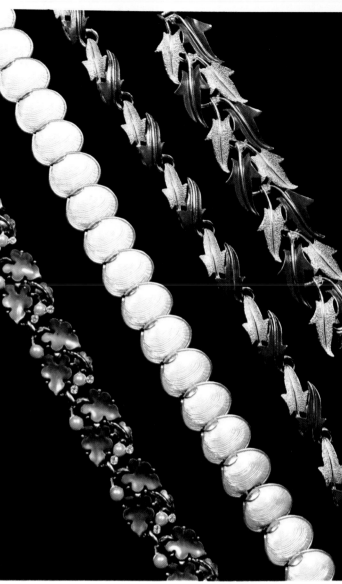

Five bracelets with charm, tailored, woven, link and strap designs made of silvertone and goldtone metal, all unmarked, circa 1950s.

Leaf and shell motifs were used to create this jewelry from the 1950s. The two piece leaf set is marked *Mode Art*.

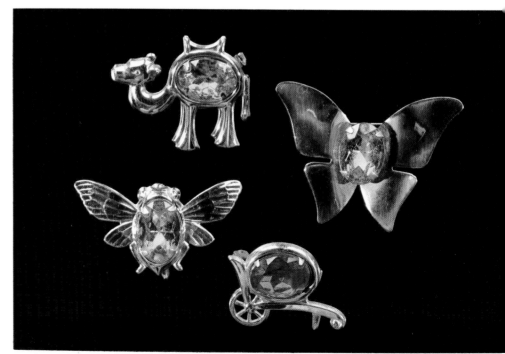

Four novelty figural pins from the 1950s.

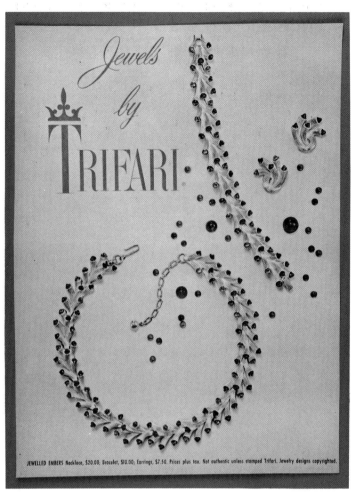

A three-piece set called "Jewelled Embers" made by *Trifari* and advertised in *Vogue* in October of 1955.

A wonderful combination of motifs and materials were used to create this set that is unfortunately unmarked. Filigree, openwork designs, serpents, mother of pearl and ruby red rhinestones were utilized in this necklace and earring set, circa 1960.

Snakeskin bracelets and earrings from the 1950s.

Leaf brooch with white enamel trim, coin and abstract pendant all made of copper, unmarked.

Cuff bracelet and matching earrings made of copper with musical motif, marked *Renoir*. Cuff bracelet with double coil design, marked *Renoir*, circa 1950s.

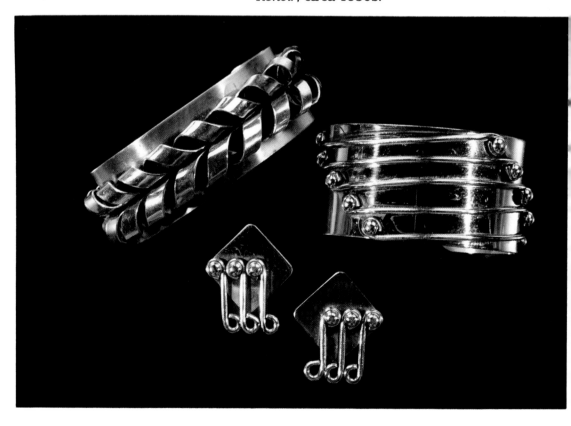

Copper

Also associated with the 1950s is a look of hand-made artisan style jewelry made of copper and enamel. Two men, one from the east coast and one from the west coast were credited with creating a style of jewelry, made of copper, that was fashionable then and extremely sought after today.

Francisco Rebajes was responsible for creating the passion for copper art work and jewelry from the late 1930s through the 1950s. From a modest beginning in Greenwich Village his business expanded enough in a few years to open a larger posh shop on Fifth Avenue in New York City. His designs included motifs drawn from abstract art, primitive African and South American culture and nature. He also produced jewelry made of sterling silver (especially in the 1940s) and used combinations of copper, silver and brass in certain designs. He dabbled in designing and producing jewelry with enamel ornamentation but credit for that must go to the genius on the west coast, Jerry Fels.

Wide segmented bracelet, stylized leaf and dove brooch all made of copper and all marked *Rebajes*.

Lariat-style necklace made of copper marked *Rebajes*. Francisco Rebajes was an artisan who became famous for his jewelry and decorative objects made of copper.

Screw-back and clip-on earrings made of copper, unmarked, circa 1950s.

Five brooches made of copper with abstract and oriental motifs, marked *Rebajes*.

Copper jewelry was extremely popular in the 1950s, largely because of the wonderful designs of Francisco Rebajes and the company Renoir. Motifs with floral and animal themes were especially liked. The five brooches pictured here, however, are unmarked.

Enamel & Paint

The company known as Renoir of California was created by a man known as Jerry Fels. Originally the firm was called "Renoir of Hollywood" but after two years in business, fire destroyed the modest business that Fels, his brother-in-law, and another close friend had created. Starting over, Fels and his brother-in-law, Curt Freiler, renamed the company, "Renoir of California." They designed and produced copper jewelry with motifs very similar to Rebajes in New York, incorporating primitive African motifs as well as geometric and abstract art themes. In 1952, the company added another line known as "Matisse, Ltd." which incorporated copper with enamel ornamentation. Musical themes, art, theater and nature were motifs most commonly used in this line. A few years later, Fels added another line to his company called the "Sauteur" line. This jewelry was made out of sterling silver and many of the same designs from the Renoir line were copied in silver. By 1960, this line, however, was eliminated.

Light blue and dark blue form the backgrounds for these unusual niello bracelets from Thailand. Instead of the typical sterling and black background, gold-plated metal with blue backgrounds were used here. Both bracelets are in their original boxes.

Bracelet, earrings and pendant all marked *Siam Sterling*. The leaf brooch is marked *Made in Thailand*, circa 1950s.

® *Evans*

ITEMS ATTRACTIVELY GIFT-BOXED
PRICES SUBJECT TO FEDERAL TAX

A fresh and ingenious new conception of costume jewelry in powdery pastel tones. Delicate contemporary classics in Evans Enamel. Decisive to the eye yet light and airy to the touch. Choice of straw, turquoise, or pastel green. Specify.

31177R941	Necklace, earrings	Retail	$16.00
31178R353	Lighter only		6.00
31179R735	Bracelet only, link		12.50
31180R735	Bracelet only, cuff		12.50

Trinkets of fashion finery created to appeal to the feminine need for vivid color accents, in luscious lipstick red Evans Enamel capped with 24K gold encrusting and beautifully complemented by the soft sheen of 14K gold electroplate. Also in royal blue or straw. Specify.

31181R735	Necklace and earrings	Retail	$12.50
31182R294	Lighter only		5.00
31183R588	Bracelet only		10.00

Turquoise, golden straw and pastel green cuff bracelets are available as single pieces or matching sets of necklace, earrings, link bracelet and lighter as shown above.

Shells by the bunch fascinatingly and fabulously combined with gold stippled tan and topaz Evans "Enamel Jewels," cling tenderly to whispy 14K gold electro plated chain in this flight of fancy. Matching cuff bracelet, earrings, and lighter complete luxurious neutral ensemble.

31184R1088	Necklace and Earrings	Retail	$18.50
31185R353	Lighter only		6.00
31186R882	Bracelet only		15.00

ROHDE-SPENCER CO., 18 SOUTH MICHIGAN AVENUE,
CHICAGO 3, ILLINOIS

Evans, best known for enameled cigarette cases, lighters and cosmetic compacts, also manufactured enameled jewelry. This wonderful assortment of necklaces, link and cuff bracelets, earrings and lighters was offered for sale in 1958.

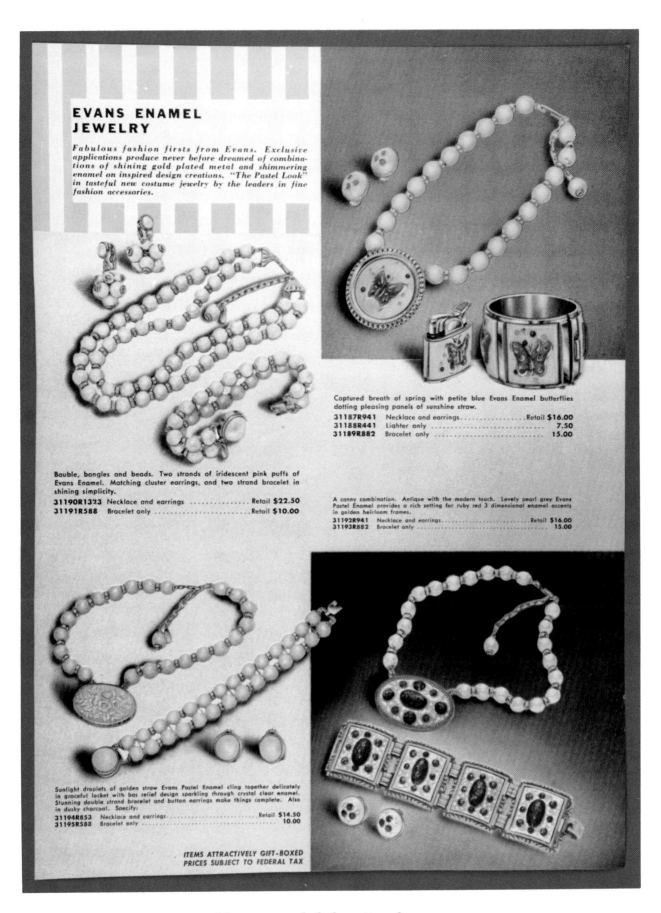

EVANS ENAMEL JEWELRY

Fabulous fashion firsts from Evans. Exclusive applications produce never before dreamed of combinations of shining gold plated metal and shimmering enamel on inspired design creations. "The Pastel Look" in tasteful new costume jewelry by the leaders in fine fashion accessories.

Captured breath of spring with petite blue Evans Enamel butterflies dotting pleasing panels of sunshine straw.

31187R941	Necklace and earrings	Retail $16.00
31188R441	Lighter only	7.50
31189R882	Bracelet only	15.00

Bauble, bangles and beads. Two strands of iridescent pink puffs of Evans Enamel. Matching cluster earrings, and two strand bracelet in shining simplicity.

31190R1323	Necklace and earrings	Retail $22.50
31191R588	Bracelet only	Retail $10.00

A canny combination. Antique with the modern touch. Lovely pearl grey Evans Pastel Enamel provides a rich setting for ruby red 3 dimensional enamel accents in golden heirloom frames.

31192R941	Necklace and earrings	Retail $16.00
31193R882	Bracelet only	15.00

Sunlight droplets of golden straw Evans Pastel Enamel cling together delicately in graceful locket with bas relief design sparkling through crystal clear enamel. Stunning double strand bracelet and button earrings make things complete. Also in dusky charcoal. Specify:

31194R853	Necklace and earrings	Retail $14.50
31195R588	Bracelet only	10.00

**ITEMS ATTRACTIVELY GIFT-BOXED
PRICES SUBJECT TO FEDERAL TAX**

More enameled favorites from
Evans popular in 1958.

Two necklace and earring sets: two-toned green plastic petals mounted in goldtone metal; two-toned pink plastic petals mounted in silvertone metal, unmarked, circa 1950s.

Small brooch in the shape of a basket, made of sterling silver, decorated with enamel and marcasites. Larger flower basket brooch is made of gilded base metal with hand-painted flowers.

Flower basket brooch and matching bracelet made of gold-plated metal, enhanced by delicate hand-painting and accented with clear rhinestones.

Lapel watches popular in 1957.

The hand-painting on this link necklace and matching screw-back earrings makes this set quite charming.

Two bracelets of the same floral design and one with a similar design were made of goldtone metal and accented with hand-painting, unmarked, circa 1950s.

Enamelled flower necklace made in the 1950s marked *Coro*.

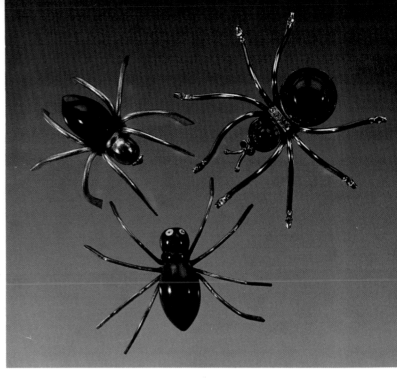

Lovely enamelled brooch made in the shape of a butterfly. Metal tag reads *Not Returnable if Removed* on one side; the opposite side reads *Lord & Taylor*.

Two lovely floral brooches, decorated with hand painting and clear rhinestones, marked *Coro*.

Three novelty pins in the shape of spiders made of silver and brass.

Figural brooch in the shape of a cat made of gold-plated sterling silver mesh, decorated with blue enamel and further embellished with genuine tiger eye, unmarked, circa 1960.

This enamelled brooch in the shape of a peacock has a clear Lucite belly.

Trio of enamelled link bracelets, all unmarked.

Pin, earrings and necklace all made of copper and enamel, unmarked, circa 1950s.

Two large link bracelets decorated with enamel and smaller segmented bracelet accented with yellow plastic rectangles, unmarked, circa 1950s.

Large link bracelet made of copper embellished with heavy enamel work in an abstract pattern, unmarked, circa 1950s.

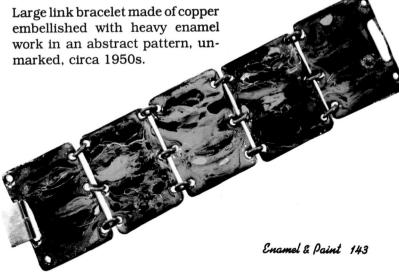

White jewelry became a fashion statement for spring and summer wear in the 1950s. Sears advertised this *Coro* jewelry in their 1955 catalog as "fashion favorites worn by the stars."

Atomic-style brooch and earring set resembling a fireworks display made of goldtone metal set with white glass beads and clear rhinestone accents marked *Alice Caviness*.

Dangle earrings and two necklaces made with white opaque glass stones accented with clear rhinestones mounted in japanned metal; opaque red glass stones mounted in goldtone metal make up the composition of the necklace at the bottom.

White

In 1930, white jewelry was a major part of the fashion scene. It was not really viewed again until around 1954 when clothing designers Dior and Balenciaga introduced white jewelry as an important feature of their new fashion collections. White opaque rhinestones were set in rhodium-plated mountings to form necklaces, bracelets and earrings. White glass and plastic beads were used to form single or multi-strand necklaces and bracelets. Choker necklaces were extremely common throughout the decade and tiny white milkglass beads were woven or braided to form intricate designs popular for spring and summer wear.

Abstract floral pin and earring set made of japanned metal and milky white glass stones, unmarked, circa 1950s.

Transparent, translucent and opaque glass stones were used to create these matched sets from the 1950s.

Choker necklace and matching cluster earrings made of round and floral-shaped milkglass beads, red glass bead tips and rhinestone rondelles, circa 1950s. White jewelry was extremely popular in the 1930s and again in the 1950s with fashion designer Balenciaga being credited with its reappearance into the world of fashion in 1953.

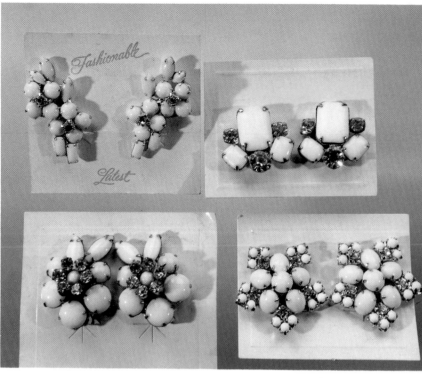

Fashionable for summer, these clip-on earrings set with milky-white glass stones and clear rhinestone accents are all unmarked.

One pair of clip-on earrings and three necklaces made of transparent and opaque glass stones.

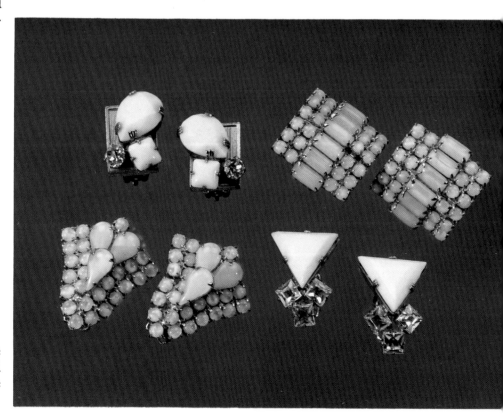

Opaque and translucent white glass stones set in goldtone metal give these earrings a summertime look.

Pearls

Cultured and simulated pearl jewelry was another 1950s favorite. Not much pearl jewelry was seen in the early 1940s during the war years but, when the war was over, interest in pearl jewelry was sparked because of the creativity of fashion designers. Long ropes of pearls as well as chokers, multi-strand necklaces, bracelets and earrings of all sorts incorporated white, off-white, champagne, pink, blue and mink-colored pearls. Companies like Deltah, Hallmark, Van Dell and Font-Asia manufactured cultured pearls while others like Coro, Bogoff, Marvella and Richelieu manufactured simulated pearl jewelry.

Thirty-two strands of simulated seed pearls with occasional crystal bead accents makes this necklace by *Vendome* a dynamic piece of jewelry.

Clip earrings made with simulated pearls and unique striped glass stones.

Necklaces and matching bracelets made of bronze-colored and smoky gray imitation pearls, circa 1950s.

Five simulated pearl bracelets with jeweled clasps, marked *Japan*.

This simulated pearl necklace becomes quite unique with the handmade, beaded, floral clasp and matching earrings marked *Japan*.

Jeweled bangle bracelet and matching earrings set with large iridescent glass stones, green rhinestones, imitation pearls and hand-painted leaves, marked *HAR*, circa 1950s.

Gold-plated brooch set with simulated pearls and colored glass stones marked *Joseph Wiesner, N. Y.*, circa 1950s.

This classic handcrafted look is achieved by the use of goldplating, simulated pearls, crystals and rhinestones. The bracelet is accompanied by its original tag bearing the name *Reynold & Helene Art Jewelry Co.* The earrings on top have patent number #2583988, circa 1952.

Large imitation pearls set in goldtone and silvertone metal embellished with clear rhinestones make these bracelets very appealing.

Jewelry that was fun to wear was fashionable throughout the 1950s. These cluster earrings with matching bracelet made of glass, pearl and metal balls are marked *Kafin*.

A combination of glass and plastic beads are cleverly utilized to create this necklace and bracelet set from the 1950s.

Necklace and matching bracelet of plastic beads, flowers and rhinestones designed for summer wear in the 1950s accompanied by original tag which reads *Jewels by Leru.*

Extremely large and heavy bracelet, silver-plated and set with large ovals of confetti Lucite, unmarked, circa 1950s.

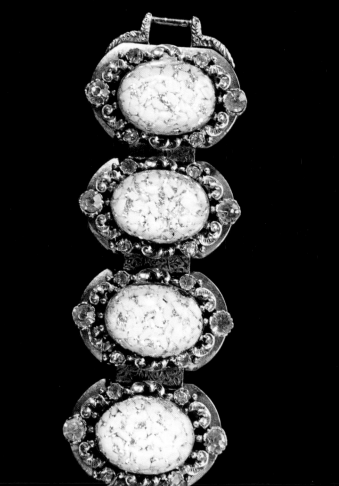

Fifties Plastics

Matched set consisting of necklace, bracelet and earrings made of goldtone metal set with shield-shaped sections of confetti Lucite, marked *Coro*, circa 1950s.

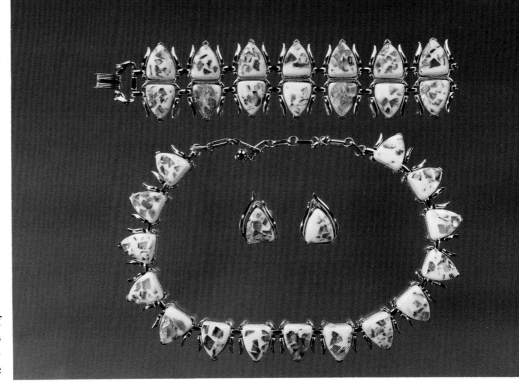

Two matched sets consisting of necklace, bracelet and earrings made of green Lucite set in gold-colored metal and purple Lucite set in silver-colored metal. This type of jewelry was extremely fashionable throughout the 1950s.

Six different examples of 1950s plastic earrings decorated with rhinestones.

Four daytime bracelets from the 1950s made of silvertone metal and multi-colored plastic.

Trio of chunky plastic charm bracelets from the 1950s.

Glass, plastic and imitation pearl beads form floral clusters which make up these bracelet and earring sets from the 1950s.

Two beaded bracelets from the 1950s. The blue bracelet is made entirely of glass beads while the green bracelet is made of plastic beads.

Necklace and bracelet made of large ovals of confetti Lucite which was all the rage during the 1950s.

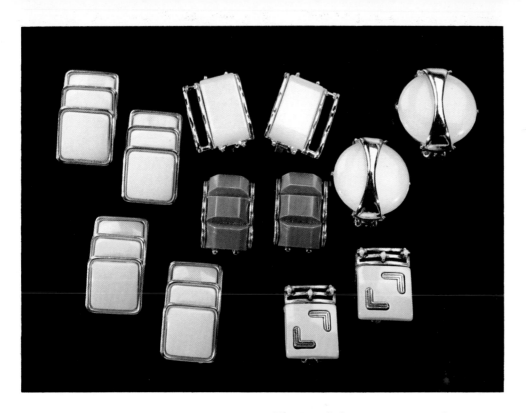

Plastic disks, squares and rectangles in various colors trimmed with goldtone metal form these six unmarked examples from the 1950s.

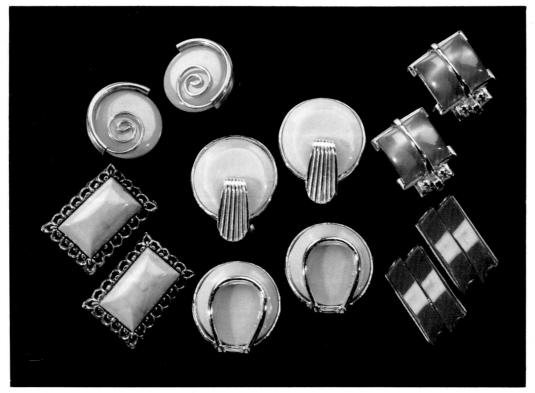

Goldtone and silvertone metal was used in conjunction with multicolored opaque plastic to create these daytime earrings from the 1950s.

Three pendants and matching earring with flowers in clear Lucite.

Three matched pin and earring sets made with flowers embedded in clear Lucite.

Melon-colored plastic was used to create the grape, rose and abstract designs for these earrings from the 1950s.

More flowers embedded in clear Lucite made into pendants with matching screw-back earrings.

Price Guide

Prices vary immensely according to an article's condition, location of the market, parts of the country, and overall quality of design. While one must make their own decisions, we can offer a guide. Jewelry in original advertisements has not been valued. The prices listed are in U.S. dollars.

Title								
page	Topaz set	125-200	p-34	Expansion bracelet	100-125		Chatelaine brooch	125-150
p-2	Flower necklace	100-125	p-35	Floral brooches	75-125 ea.	p-57	Figural brooch	100-150
p-3	Revival demi-parure	250-300	p-36	Daisy set	125-150		Alex Carole mask pin	75-100
p-5	Trifari basket clip	200-300		Leaf necklace	125-150		Mazer mask clip	400-500
	Dress clip	175-250		Floral brooches	75-125		Winged knight	200-250
p-6	Clip	150-225	p-37	Floral brooch	150-200	p-58	Charm bracelet	300-400
	Brooch	175-250		Basket brooch	100-125		Segmented bracelet	65-85
p-7	Scarab bracelet	350-450	p-38	Circle brooch	75-100	p-59	CoroCraft fox	450-550
p-10	Coro bracelet	50-75		Clip	75-100		Bird of Paradise	400-450
	Coro choker necklace	75-100		Floral brooch	75-100		Necklace	80-100
p-11	Trifari earrings	75-100		Large stylized brooch	500-600	p-60	Haskell bracelet	250-300
p-12	Mazer set	275-325		Three stylized			Flower earrings	20-40 pair
p-13	Van Dell set	175-225		brooches	175-300 ea.	p-61	Plastic earrings	20-40 pair
	with original box	225-250	p-39	Floral brooch	100-145		Necklace and bracelet	125-150 set
	Brass choker	50-75	p-40	Floral brooch	125-150	p-62	Brooch	125-150
	Bracelet	45-65		Trifari snowflake	125-175		Necklace	175-225
p-15	Lapel watch	300-400	p-41	Sterling necklace	135-185		Bracelet	150-175
	Watch/locket	250-300	p-42	Three floral brooches	60-125 ea.		Large bird brooch	125-150
p-16	Bracelet & Earring Set	200-300		Large bow brooch	85-110	p-63	Figural brooch	200-250
	Dorsons' set	300-400		Sterling scissors	60-90		Ring	50-90
	Strap bracelet	175-225		Two stylized brooches	125-175		Earrings	65-95 pair
	Flexible bracelet	125-175	p-44	Stylized floral spray	175-225		Bracelet	175-225
p-17	Choker necklaces	25-75 ea.		Sterling earrings	75-100 pair	p-64	Three piece set	200-300
	Crescent earrings	75-125		Blossom brooch	125-150		Grape necklace	125-150
	Parure	250-300		Large floral brooch	450-550		Bracelet	175-225
p-18	Parure	350-450	p-45	Three piece set in box	100-125	p-69	Necklace	150-200
	Gold-filled brooches	40-90 ea.		CoroCraft brooch	200-300	p-70	Bracelets	75-125 ea.
	Flower brooch	150-200		Two stylized brooches	100-150	p-73	Tree brooch	150-175
	Circular brooch	100-125	p-46	Gold-plated brooch	125-175		Leaf brooch	175-225
p-19	Heart brooch	75-100		Three piece set	100-125	p-75	Necklace & brooch	150-200 set
	Hat and cane brooch	80-100		with original box	125-150		Mazer set	225-275 set
	Clip	65-85		Faux emerald brooch	125-175		Regency necklace	225-300
p-22	Duette	175-225	p-47	Coro brooch	150-200	p-76	Weiss set	300-400
	Brooch	100-140		Stylized brooch	175-225		Cathe set	175-200
p-23	Chatelaine pin sets	150-200		Iskin set	175-200		Unmarked set	125-150
	with original boxes	200-225		with original box	200-225	p-78	Sterling rhinestone set	200-300
p-24	Vogue brooch	200-300	p-49	Stylized leaf, flower			Center parure	150-200
p-25	Bracelet & earring set	175-225		and bow brooches	75-125 ea.		Donna set	75-125
	Eisenberg Original	500-600		Floral brooch	200-250	p-80	Expansion bracelet	75-125
	Austrian crystal			Earrings	75-100 pair		Earrings	20-45 pair
	brooches	300-400 ea.		Three sterling brooches	125-175 ea.	p-81	Earrings	40-75 pair
p-26	Pewter-like brooch	75-125	p-50	Bow brooch	175-200	p-82	Five bracelets	100-150 ea.
	Figural scatter pins	150-200 set		Trifari brooch	200-300		Pink bracelet	65-95
p-27	Deer brooch	250-350	p-51	Crown set	75-95		Jomaz bracelet	75-125
	Leaf brooches	100-150 ea.	p-53	Figural pins:			Floral bracelet	70-90
	Aquamarine brooch	75-125		Seahorse	60-85	p-83	Brooch & earring set	75-125
p-28	Three piece set	125-175		Horse set	75-100		Earrings	40-85 pair
p-29	Tailored earrings	25-50 pair		Swordfish set	75-100	p-84	Rhinestone earrings	50-100 pair
p-30	Brass & glass necklaces:			Lovebirds	65-95	p-85	Pin & earring set	65-85
	Left	125-175		Coro Duette set	200-300		Two brooches	70-90 ea.
	Right	200-300		Horsehead pins	90-140	p-86	Judy Lee set	150-200
	Abstract floral pins	65-95 set	p-54	Coin earrings	25-45 pair		Four brooches	75-100 ea.
	Bracelet & earring set	150-225		Lovebird set	95-145		Three atomic brooches	75-125 ea.
p-31	Bracelets	100-200 ea.		Sterling slippers	85-135		Three rhinestone pins	100-150 ea.
p-32	Earrings	25-45	p-55	Sterling hand pins	60-125 ea.	p-87	Parure by King	300-400
p-33	Napier chain jewelry:			Pin and earring set	65-85		Pin & earring set	125-175
	Bracelet	45-75		Bug pins	60-90 ea.		Atomic brooches	75-125 ea.
	Necklaces	60-90 ea.		Peacock set	100-150	p-88	Six brooches	75-125 ea.
	Large tailored		p-56	Trifari sword pin	100-150		Two pin & earring sets	95-145 set
	earrings	35-65 pair		Center sword pin	45-60		Three rhinestone pins	100-150 ea.
	Button earrings	20-40 pair		Sword pin & earring set	150-200	p-89	Smoky gray earrings	50-100 pair
				Two Coro pins	125-175 ea.		Black glass earrings	45-90 pair

p-90	Weiss necklaces	125-175 ea.
	Four piece set	200-225
	Necklace	125-150
p-91	Pell set	125-150
	Floral pin & earring set	125-200
	Diamond-shaped brooch	85-135
	Bracelet & earring sets	100-200 set
p-92	Bracelet & earring sets	100-200 set
	Necklace & bracelet set	125-225 set
	Earrings	50-90 pair
p-93	Lucien set	150-225
	Weiss set	200-300
	Earrings	50-100 pair
p-94	Earrings (green)	30-60 pair
	Earrings (topaz)	50-90 pair
p-95	Pin & earring sets	100-150 set
	Earrings	55-85 pair
p-96	Necklaces	125-225 ea.
	Pin & earring sets	100-175 set
p-97	Bellini set	300-400
	Schreiner set	250-300
	Unmarked sets	100-150 ea.
p-98	Pin & earring set	100-150 set
	Earrings	45-90 pair
	Coro set	125-150 set
p-99	Florenza earrings	40-65 pair
	Regency brooch	100-125
	Wolcott set	150-200
	Beaded earrings	50-75 pair
p-100	Bracelet & earring set	175-225
	Top pin & earring sets	100-150 set
	Center pin & earring set	125-175
	Florenza set	175-225
p-101	Pin & earring sets	100-150 set
	Earrings	50-90 pair
	Karu pin	75-90
	Lisner earrings	45-70
p-102	Necklace & bracelet	200-250
	Necklace & earring set	150-175
	Bracelets	75-150 ea.
p-103	Bracelets & earring sets	125-175 set
	Translucent sets	140-190 set
	Faceted glass bracelets	225-275 ea.
	with earrings	300-325 set
p-104	Glass earrings	30-60 pair
	Glass beads & earrings	50-90 set
p-105	Necklace & earrings	70-100 set
	Bracelet & earring sets	75-100 set
p-106	Crystal set	100-125
	Earrings	50-75 pair
	De Mario set	350-400
p-107	Bracelet & earring sets	100-150 set
p-108	Aventurine set	150-200
	Necklace	250-300
	Bracelet & earrings	100-150
p-109	Necklace & earring set	85-135
	Necklace	250-300
	Bracelets	75-100 ea.
p-110	Parure	300-350
	Necklace & earring set	125-150
	Earrings	50-90 pair
p-111	Demi-parure	250-325
	Bracelets	60-90 ea.
p-112	Bracelet & earring set	100-150
	Grape set by King	100-150
	Necklace & earring sets	50-75 set
p-113	Juliana set	150-200

	De Mario set	250-300
	Necklace & bracelet	200-250
	Bracelet & earring sets	125-175 set
p-114	Necklace & earring set	150-200
	Two choker necklaces	150-200 ea.
	Two bracelets	250-300 ea.
p-115	Parure	300-400
	Schauer sets	200-300 ea.
	Earrings	40-100 pair
p-116	Earrings	50-85 pair
	Necklace & earring set	200-250
	Two brooches	95-135 ea.
p-117	Judy Lee set	200-300
	Two brooches	80-120 ea.
	Bracelet & earring set	125-175
p-118	Three necklaces	75-100 ea.
	Butterfly brooch	125-175
	Earrings	40-90 pair
p-119	Boucher set	300-400
	Butterfly brooch	100-125
	Turtle brooch	125-150
	Two stylized brooches	85-125 ea.
	Pin & earring set	75-125
p-120	Parure	200-250
	Bracelets	125-175 ea.
	Brooches	65-125 ea.
p-121	Necklace & bracelet set	175-225
	Link necklaces	125-175 ea.
	Three brooches	150-200 ea.
p-122	Wiesner sets	125-175 set
	Choker necklaces	50-100 ea.
	Earrings	65-95 pair
p-123	Earrings	35-85 pair
	Necklace	75-100
	Two brooches	50-75
	Lucite sets	100-150 set
p-124	Four piece set	225-300
	Marbleized sets	200-250
	Earrings	40-75 pair
p-125	Earrings	45-90 pair
	Bracelets	100-175 ea.
	HAR set	150-200
p-126	Three bracelets	75-100 ea.
	Four bracelets	100-200 ea.
	Earrings	45-90 pair
p-127	Pin & earring set	100-125
	Five bracelets	50-100 ea.
	Six bracelets	60-125 ea.
	Earrings	50-90 pair
p-128	Necklace & bracelet set	175-225
	Brooch	50-100
	Bracelet & earring sets	150-200 set
	Bracelets	75-100 ea.
p-129	Napier set	200-250
	Link set	100-150
p-130	Choker necklaces	50-75 ea.
	Earrings (top right)	50-90 pair
	Earrings (bottom)	40-100
p-131	Coro set	175-200
	Coro bracelet with box	65-90
		100
p-132	Five bracelets	40-75 ea.
	Mode Art set	85-125
	Shell choker	35-65
	Leaf choker	35-75
	Novelty pins	25-45 ea.
p-133	Necklace & earring set	200-300

	Snakeskin bracelets	100-125
	with earrings	125-150
p-134	Leaf brooch	40-60
	Pendants	50-85
	Cuff bracelet	50-75
	Renoir set	100-150
p-135	Necklace	125-175
	Bracelet	125-175
	Bird brooch	45-75
	Leaf brooch	55-90
p-136	Earrings	25-50 pair
	Brooches	50-100 ea.
p-137	Bracelets in box	125-175 ea.
	Earrings	50-100 pair
	Pendant	75-125
	Bracelet	100-125
p-140	Necklace & earring sets	100-125 ea.
	Basket pins	100-150 ea.
	Bracelet & brooch set	125-150
p-141	Necklace & earring set	75-100
	Bracelets	65-95 ea.
	Coro necklace	100-125
p-142	Butterfly brooch	50-100
	Spider pins	75-125 ea.
	Cat pin	150-200
	Flower pins	75-125 ea.
	Peacock pin	100-125
p-143	Enamelled link bracelets	65-95 ea.
	Large link bracelets	75-125 ea.
	Earrings	20-40 pair
	Necklace	75-100
	Abstract copper bracelet	150-200
p-144	Caviness set	200-300
	Earrings	45-65
	Necklaces	100-150 ea.
p-145	Bracelet & earring sets	125-175 set
	Pin & earring set	75-100
	Necklace and earrings	75-100
p-146	Necklaces	125-175 ea.
	Earrings	50-85 pair
p-147	Vendome necklace	175-225
	Earrings	45-75 pair
	Necklace & bracelet sets	100-125 set
p-148	Bracelets	50-100 ea.
	Necklace & earrings	75-125
	Bracelet & earring set	125-150
	Brooch	125-175
p-149	Top bracelet	175-225
	Earrings	75-100 pair
	Bracelets	75-150 ea.
	Bracelet & earring sets	125-150
p-150	Top flower set	175-225
	Leru set	150-200
	Bracelet	125-175
p-151	Coro set	125-200
	Bottom sets	100-125
p-152	Earrings	40-85 pair
	Charm bracelets	75-150 ea.
	Bracelets	65-100 ea.
p-153	Bracelet & earring sets	100-125 set
	Bracelets	85-145 ea.
p-154	Earrings	40-90 pair
	Lucite sets	75-100
p-155	Lucite sets	75-100

Index

About the Author

Roseann Ettinger is a leading vintage jewelry and clothing dealer with twenty years experience studying clothing style and design. She is also the author of *Popular Jewelry 1840-1940*, *Handbags*, and *Compacts and Smoking Accessories*. Mrs. Ettinger owns the shop *Remember When* at 16 South Wyoming Street, Hazelton, Pennsylvania where she can be contacted to answer questions about this interesting period of fashion and accessories.